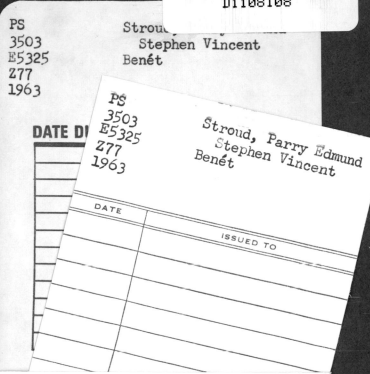

Twayne's United States Authors Series

Sylvia E. Bowman, *Editor*

INDIANA UNIVERSITY

Stephen Vincent Benét

STEPHEN VINCENT BENÉT

by PARRY STROUD

Washburn University of Topeka

 27

Twayne Publishers, Inc.   ::   New York

To Dorothy

Preface

STEPHEN VINCENT BENÉT, in his Invocation to *John Brown's Body*, describes his pursuit of the elusive American Muse and his three moments of communion with her. Divinity reveals herself to man in fleeting glimpses, and the American Muse (not to be confused with well-draped, statuesque ladies with passports from Greece, Rome, or England) has been swifter than the mind's eye of most writers. Among the poets, Walt Whitman sensed her first and most often, seeing her mystically flying across the continent and rearing a race of large-souled men and women. Carl Sandburg has witnessed her smoky glories over Chicago streets and in prairie haze. Hart Crane dreamed of her moving across a bridge spanning time, space, and culture, though she vanished in the mists of his private despairs. For the prose-poet Thomas Wolfe, the Muse rode a midnight express hurtling across the land he loved.

Each of these writers' visions has a distinction worth the reader's own pursuit, whether his primary aim be art or love of his country. Benét in his Invocation defers to the wisdom of those who recognize no nation but Art, but his best writing testifies to his own wisdom in forming his palette from the varied colors of American history. The self-knowledge and beauty which Americans can find in his work constitute a literary resource which the nation may draw upon through the rest of this century and beyond.

In the prolonged national struggle not merely for survival but for the world's liberty, all of our literature which deals with the national soul becomes doubly important. Its significance may come from a prophetic vision of national greatness based on freedom and responsibility and love of man. Its meaning may arise out of a tragic sense of national failure, such as a perversion of or falling away from national ideals. Such a sense of deep concern for the nation may express itself through a judgment of the present by the greatness of the past, through a reference to the present by means of the past, or through a prophecy seeking to alter the present national course by warning of possible disaster. Or this literature of patriotism may perform all three of these services. Sandburg's *The People, Yes* and Benét's *John Brown's Body* are examples of such a work: they are epics which summon up part of the national heritage, show its importance for the present, and look to the future.

The potential worth of such a literature is attested to by classics of world literature. The epics of Homer link the destiny of two city-states and an island kingdom to the will of the gods. Like the Greeks, the Hindus have two great epics woven of legend, myth, and history: *The Mahabharata* and *The Ramayana*, both written in the centuries preceding the Christian era. Vergil's *Aeneid* sings of the wanderings of its epic hero from the fall of Troy to the founding of Rome. Vergil appears as Dante's guide in *The Divine Comedy*, the great medieval religious epic, which is in some ways a pre-national epic. A century earlier the *Chanson de Roland* had sung of a tragic French defeat in Spain. Ariosto's *Orlando Furioso* is a fine Italian version of the same story. The *Lusiads* of Luís de Camoëns is an epic telling of the adventures of Vasco de Gama as a representative of the Portuguese nation. Spenser's *Faerie Queene* on one level of allegory records the politics of England under Elizabeth. Shakespeare's historical plays are, on one serious level, studies in the nature of the ideal king and the stable state. Five of the six great tragedies are also tragedies of states whose foundations are shaken by the passions of their rulers. In the nineteenth century the novel displaced the epic as the genre for the national theme, notably in Russia, where Tolstoy's *War and Peace* told of the Napoleonic invasion. Dostoevsky's *Crime and Punishment* and *The Brothers Karamazov*, though primarily concerned with individual salvation, deal also with the destiny and soul of Russia, as does the recent distinguished novel of Boris Pasternak. The literature of nationalism has an ancient and honorable history not yet ended. The soul of a nation is not the greatest theme—man's relation to God or the universe or man's relation to his whole age are greater themes—but it is worthy of the greatest writer.

Our own American literature, which concerns itself primarily with the state of the nation, has since the Civil War been overshadowed by a literature of alienation and by a criticism which has been increasingly concerned with aesthetics. The troubled expatriatism of Henry James, the embracing of aristocracy, classicism, and Anglicanism by T. S. Eliot, and the weird treasons of Ezra Pound are merely the best-known instances of the cleavage between the American writer and the American culture. Less extreme but nonetheless relevant are the cases of Stephen Crane, F. Scott Fitzgerald, and Ernest Hemingway as intermittent exiles. In another category is a writer like John Dos Passos, whose long, bitter fictional disillusion with the U. S. A. perhaps conceals at bottom a deep love not wholly frustrated.

The problem of the writer in post-Civil War America—which is merely an aspect of the problem of the artist in other fields—has as many terms as an astrophysical equation, and it cannot be analyzed in a preface to another work. I wish, however, to set forth some ideas bearing on this problem because they underlie or enter directly into this study of Benét.

First of all, the problem of the alienation of the artist from American society is merely the domestic manifestation of a universal problem. The gravity of the domestic problem has perhaps been exaggerated; certainly most important American writers have accommodated themselves to life here, and many have thrived. The Angry Young Men of Britain and the earlier flight from England to America of W. H. Auden and Stephen Spender suggest that the writer anywhere, being more sensitive, more intelligent, and more idealistic than most of his fellow citizens, is apt to be more sharply critical of his nation. At its most terrible, however, the thwarting of the artist is not merely psychological, social, economic, or cultural—but political. The absolutisms of the twentieth century have silenced many writers, through murder or fear, and have corrupted others. It follows that the writer must seek not only his own individual freedom but also the universality of freedom upon which the artist's freedom depends.

On the other hand, although the writer in America should actively support through his spoken words and actions the extension of freedom, he should not be placed under any compulsion to enlist his talents in the service of democracy—to write, say, novels contrasting the blessings of freedom with the horrors of communism. Such a novel might be readable, but if a writer's genius does not lie in this direction, he should not force himself along it, nor should the least external pressure be applied to him through criticism or any other means. Benét had the wisdom and largeness of spirit to take this position even in wartime, despite his almost complete devotion to the writing of propaganda.

The almost certain prospect of a struggle with communism lasting into the next century—providing that a universal holocaust does not impose the peace of death—raises a danger that patriotism could create critical blindness. Edgar Allan Poe rightly decried the tendency to praise a stupid book merely because its stupidity is American. The rise of ultrapatriotic groups since World War II has already demonstrated the degree to which the clarity of reason may be fogged by political zealotry. The commendable, even necessary, search for sources of American cultural strength must stop short of censorship and the exaltation of all things American. In the end such extremism brings debility, not strength.

However, recognition of the truth that literature must ultimately justify itself as literature should not obscure the equally important truth that literature has meaning. The writer has a moral responsibility as well as an artistic one, and he may shirk neither. The meanings of literature are the meanings of life at one or more removes, and merely to look at life or to live with either aesthetic or moral detachment is to betray life. The effort to condone the fascism, the treason, and the anti-Semitism of Ezra Pound should shock a lively moral sensibility so that it cannot applaud the beauties of his poetry. The simultaneous attempt to mildly condemn an anti-Semitic passage while admiring its metrical virtuosity represents a perilous critical schizophrenia. If we have collectively become so enfeebled in our moral and political judgments, so entangled in a slack relativism that we cannot say with certainty that fascism, treason, and anti-Semitism are wrong, however embellished with artistry they may be, then we are lost in an ethical jungle. Every true liberal and every true conservative knows that both fascism and communism are hostile to the creative spirit. The democratic critic should condemn both in literature. He should also evaluate the style and structure through which they are represented. But to disregard meaning is to place art above life.

Put in extreme terms, a separation of meaning and literary form becomes absurd. No one can praise a hack's liberal ideas and then take him to task for limping meters and banal metaphors. To a considerable extent the liberal ideas are debased by the style. One school of thought holds that the style and meaning are inseparable, but this concept renders comprehensive criticism impossible. The problem approaches a metaphysical complexity and offers a fertile sphere for error. A certain type of critic is apt to find himself so beguiled by complexity of form and arresting manner that he forgets that literature is also a criticism of life. A disciple of Vernon Parrington is apt to find himself so fascinated by a developing liberalism that he overlooks the concomitant lack of art.

Liberal criticism needs redefinition today, not merely because Lionel Trilling has seriously challenged some of its assumptions in *The Liberal Imagination*[1] (1950), but because any philosophy needs constant invigoration and constant re-examination of its tenets. I am not suggesting that liberalism is an intellectual Paul Bunyan of literature, but I believe that it offers fruitful approaches to some types of literature. American political liberalism, which has won the allegiance of many writers throughout our history and which in its various forms has infused our most dynamic periods, has also, I believe, definite connections with liberal religion as well as liberal criticism. These interrelationships perhaps resemble those which have developed between conservatism, the New Criticism, and Christianity during recent decades.

No metaphysical definition of liberalism exists to be uncovered by however prolonged a meditation, but certain broad concepts and attitudes seem to me to characterize American liberalism in its literary manifestations. I suggest first of all that liberalism believes in the pursuit of life, liberty, and happiness; to this extent it is an optimistic philosophy. But although it stresses the possibilities for goodness in man, it realistically recognizes his inventive wickedness and laughs at his follies. Liberalism believes in the primacy of the individual within the bounds of social responsibility; and, to the extent that it sees his rights as having a metaphysical sanction, it is a transcendental philosophy. Liberalism is distrustful of dogma; it is tolerant, experimental, pragmatic, and eclectic. Libertarian and humanitarian as it is, it rejects deterministic and mechanistic philosophies of man and society, though since the Civil War it has had a healthy regard for social forces. American liberalism justifies its patriotism not primarily as love of native land but as love of freedom and justice; and it has a far hope for the world's freedom. The basic spirit of liberalism is reverence for life, to borrow the fine phrase of Albert Schweitzer.

The liberalism of Stephen Vincent Benét was evidenced politically through his steadfast support of Franklin Delano Roosevelt and the principal measures, domestic and international, of the New Deal. Benét's final years were devoted to fighting World War II on the propaganda front, the only one on which his age, physical condition, and family responsibilities permitted him to fight. He fought with sharp, sometimes tragic awareness of America's shortcomings, yet his love for his country was sustained by his vision and knowledge of her as defender of the world's liberty. Benét's literary liberalism was reflected in many ways: in, for example, the catholicity of his tastes, by his refusal to regard the writing of wartime propaganda as a duty to be imposed on all writers, in his constant concern with the individual, and, most importantly, by the central drift of his writing toward the American theme.

The elucidation of Benét's liberalism as it appears in his writings is of course one of my major objectives in this study. His liberalism and patriotism nourished each other and infused his finest work, and I have sought to explain how they do so. Not all of his writings were so shaped, however, and I have dealt with these works by means of critical approaches that seemed appropriate. I have also attempted to place Benét in rough historical and literary perspective, to show his relationship with his own time at the major points of contact, and to connect him with the main currents of American literature which flow through his work.

Besides pointing to the historical and cultural bearings of Benét's writings, I have aimed at scrutinizing consistently the quality of his interpretation of his themes. Here I must acknowledge a debt to the New Critics, too numerous to identify, who have permanently established the importance of close reading. The connotations of a word, the appropriateness of a meter, the implications of a symbol, the architectural complexities of a novel are aspects of literary criticism that distinguished New Critics have taught us how to handle. In my consideration of Benét's poetry and novels in particular and to a lesser extent in his short stories, I have sought to make profitable use of the exacting techniques of one of the most vital critical movements of the twentieth century. At the same time I have tried to avoid certain New Critical pitfalls: the confusion of microscopy with insight, of jargon with erudition, of symbolism with importance, of cultism with divine election.

Since I could not discuss all of Benét's writings, I decided to examine to a degree proportionate to their excellence those works which have seemed to me most important. These are mostly his best works, of course; but I have also attempted to say enough about his second- or third-rate work to provide a fairly complete conception of the whole body of his writing. I have had to pass over the majority of Benét's numerous minor poems and short stories, and the admirer of Benét may find that I have said nothing at all about a favorite poem or story. I have, however, appraised representative poems and short stories, as well as virtually all of Benét's work in other genres. Some of his radio dramas and the two operas for which he wrote librettos I have not discussed because they are on the periphery of my central literary concerns. My choices for critical analysis have also been partially guided by considerations of availability: whenever possible I have selected writings which an interested reader may find without difficulty. One important exception is Benét's best novel, *James Shore's Daughter,* which is unfortunately out of print and likely to remain so.

One of the problems of the critic is to disentangle his literary judgments from his personal judgments of writers. I do not know that I have succeeded in doing this. Stephen Vincent Benét seems to me to have been an admirable and engaging man in every respect. Not the least of his endearing qualities was his inability to take himself too seriously as a writer, despite his generally serious purposes. If sometimes a boy read parts of *John Brown's Body* to his girl until he found kissing better, Benét would, he thought, be satisfied with his posthumous fame.[1] Like his William Sycamore, he would have much content in his dying to know that one admirer of *John Brown's Body* is the President of the United States.[2]

I wish to record my gratitude to the Yale University Press for generous permission to draw liberally upon Charles A. Fenton's *Stephen Vincent Benét* and upon *Selected Letters of Stephen Vincent Benét,* edited by Mr. Fenton. Lines from Benét's poems "The Hemp" and "The Mountain Whippoorwill" are quoted with the permission of Holt, Rinehart, and Winston, Inc. I am particularly grateful to Benét's agents, Brandt and Brandt, for consenting to my use of the numerous quotations from his other works.

In writing this study I have been given valuable help. To my wife, Dorothy, who read my manuscript, I am indebted for a continuation of that same critical sensitivity and sound judgment she displayed as my brightest graduate student. To Sylvia Bowman I am grateful for editorial patience and understanding enduring past several deadlines, for alert spotting of errors, and for many wise suggestions for improving my manuscript.

PARRY STROUD

Washburn University of Topeka
Topeka, Kansas
January 30, 1962

Contents

Chronology

The biographical dates and events listed in this chronological table are based upon the Calendar in *Selected Letters of Stephen Vincent Benét*, edited by Charles A. Fenton (Yale University Press, 1960), and upon Charles A. Fenton, *Stephen Vincent Benét: The Life and Times of an American Man of Letters, 1898-1943* (Yale University Press, 1958). Titles of publications and other bibliographical information appear as recorded in Gladys L. Maddocks, "Stephen Vincent Benét: A Bibliography," *Bulletin of Bibliography and Dramatic Index,* XX (September, 1951—April, 1952).

1898   Stephen Vincent is born July 22 in Bethlehem, Pa., the third child and the second son of James Walker Benét, Captain of Ordnance, United States Army, and Frances Neill Rose Benét. Laura and William Rose are Stephen's sister and brother.

1899   Benét family moves to Watervliet (N.Y.) Arsenal.

1904   Major Benét and family at Rock Island (Illinois) Arsenal.

1905   Benét family moves to Benicia (California) Arsenal.

1910-1911   Stephen attends military academy at San Rafael, California.

1911   Benét family, including Stephen, moves to Augusta (Georgia) Arsenal.

1911-1915   Stephen attends coeducational academy in Augusta.

1915   Makes first professional sale of a poem, to *New Republic*. Enters Yale College. Publishes *Five Men and Pompey*, his first book of poems.

1916   Elected to editorial board of *Yale Literary Magazine*.

1918   Elected chairman of *Yale Literary Magazine*. After completing junior year, leaves school to enlist in the Army. Honorably discharged because of bad eyesight. *Young*

Adventure (poems) published. Works briefly for State Department in Washington.

1919 Re-enters Yale; granted B. A. degree in June. After working for a few months as advertising copywriter in New York, enters Yale Graduate School. As a member of Henry Seidel Canby's writing course, begins work on novel.

1920 Awarded M. A. degree by Yale. Granted a traveling fellowship by Yale. Goes to Paris and completes *The Beginning of Wisdom*, his first novel. Meets Rosemary Carr.

1921 Becomes engaged to Miss Carr. Returns to United States. Married in Chicago. The Benéts return to Europe for honeymoon.

1922 Returns to New York with wife. "The Ballad of William Sycamore" appears in *New Republic*. Second novel, *Young People's Pride*, published.

1923 "King David" awarded *Nation's* poetry prize. *Jean Huguenot* (novel).

1924 Birth of Benéts' first child, Stephanie Jane.

1925 "The Mountain Whippoorwill" (*Century Magazine*). *Tiger Joy* (poems).

1926 *Spanish Bayonet* (novel). Receives Guggenheim Fellowship and goes to Paris with wife and daughter. Works on *John Brown's Body*. Son, Thomas Carr, born in Paris.

1927 Guggenheim Fellowship extended for six months.

1928 Colonel Benét dies in Pennsylvania. *John Brown's Body* published.

1929 Receives Pulitzer Prize for poetry. Returns to United States with family. Elected to National Institute of Arts and Letters.

1929- Does script-writing in Hollywood for three months.
1930

1931 Daughter, Rachel, born in New York.

1933 *A Book of Americans*, in collaboration with Rosemary Carr Benét. Accepts editorship of Yale Series of Younger Poets competition.

1934 *James Shore's Daughter* (novel).

1935 Begins regular reviewing for New York *Herald Tribune* and *Saturday Review of Literature*. First two "Nightmare" poems in *New Yorker*. "Ode to Walt Whitman" in *SRL*.

1936 "Notes to Be Left in a Cornerstone," *New Yorker*. *Burning City* (poems). "The Devil and Daniel Webster" (*Saturday Evening Post*) awarded O. Henry Memorial Prize for best American short story of year.

1937 "Daniel Webster and the Sea Serpent" and "Johnny Pye and the Fool-Killer." Latter story republished as O. Henry Memorial Prize story. *Thirteen O'Clock* (short stories). Awarded honorary degree by Yale.

1938 "Into Egypt" and "Jacob and the Indians," *Saturday Evening Post*. Elected to American Academy of Arts and Letters.

1939 *The Devil and Daniel Webster*, operetta with libretto by Benét and music by Douglas Moore, produced in New York by American Lyric Theatre. Benét hospitalized several weeks for nervous breakdown caused by overwork. *Tales Before Midnight* (short stories).

1940 "Freedom's a Hard-Bought Thing" awarded O. Henry Memorial Prize as best American short story of year. "We Stand United" read by Raymond Massey over CBS at Carnegie Hall rally sponsored by Council for Democracy.

1941 "Listen to the People" (poetic radio script) published by *Life* and read over NBC prior to address by President Roosevelt. Benét in general poor health but continues propaganda activities on behalf of democracy.

1942 *Selected Works* (2 vols.) chosen as Book of the Month Club selection. *A Child Is Born, Dear Adolf, They Burned the Books* (radio scripts). *All That Money Can Buy*, a film version by Benét of "The Devil and Daniel Webster." Benét's "Prayer" read by President Roosevelt at United Nations ceremonies.

1943 Dies on March 13 in the arms of his wife, following a heart attack. *Western Star* (first part of a projected companion epic for *John Brown's Body*).

1944 Awarded Pulitzer Prize for poetry. *America* (short history) translated into many languages for distribution in Europe and Asia.

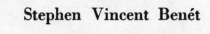Stephen Vincent Benét

CHAPTER 1

The Minor Poetry: History, Love, Laughter, and Prophecy

STEPHEN VINCENT BENÉT was first a poet, and he remained essentially a poet throughout his career, although he disciplined himself into becoming a skilled writer of short stories, novels, and radio scripts.[1] His poetry has five major modes: the dramatic monologue; the ballad; the lyric; the prophetic; and the epic. Something of a national poet in the tradition of Whitman and Sandburg, Benét was, like Whitman, fundamentally a romantic poet, but in different ways and to considerably less consequence. Lacking Whitman's transcendental faith and philosophy, Benét was unable to give his poetry an overall unity, and his romanticism was refracted and fragmented. *John Brown's Body*[2] aside, Benét was a minor poet, though his unfinished *Western Star* (1943) must be reckoned with in gauging his potential stature. The nature and quality of Benét's poetic achievement have not yet been fully analyzed, despite a number of vigorous and perceptive reviews.

No discussion of Benét's poetry can go very far without entering the vexed and murky domains of the controversy over modern poetry. The placing of him in the romantic tradition of course takes him out of the neo-metaphysical tradition which is central in modern poetry. Irony sharpens a good many of Benét's poems, and he often deals with the modern world; but his is not a difficult poetry of wit or of startling juxtapositions all compact of symbolism. Benét's tastes were catholic, but he followed his own genius, and its roots were in the nineteenth century rather than in the seventeenth. Yet at his best he was a modern poet of his own sort.

Basil Davenport has pointed to the major components of

Benét's romanticism: his fascination with the remote in time and place, his sense of the macabre, his sensitive awareness of landscape.[3] To these qualities should be added Benét's concern with emotion, with states of mind, rather than with ideas. His poetry is also vivid in its imagery, richly colored like that of many romantics. In this respect he resembles the nineteenth-century English poet, designer, and craftsman whose work most shaped Benét's poetry: William Morris.[4] Benét used the ballad form after the manner of Morris, and the octosyllabic couplets that Morris employed in some of his long narrative poems reappear in some of Benét's poems. Morris' technique of weaving song into narrative was paralleled by Benét in his two epics.

I *Five Men and Pompey*

Benét's first published book of poems, however, owed more to Robert Browning than to Morris. *Five Men and Pompey* (Boston, 1915) is a series of dramatic monologues spoken by Roman leaders on the eve of Caesar's accession to imperial power. Although the basic form derives from Browning, Benét gave his half-dozen portraits a collective significance of his own in that they trace the fall of the Roman Republic. In this way they herald Benét's *John Brown's Body,* some eleven years later, except that the American historical poem deals with the sundering and then the forging of a republic.

Benét himself regarded *Five Men and Pompey* as significant not only as the beginning of his poetic career, but as germinating the form of *John Brown's Body.*[5] Quite justifiably, he also saw it as superior to much of his work done in the early 1920's. The merit of *Five Men and Pompey* rests upon skillful characterization through the difficult form of the dramatic monologue, upon the successful introduction of dramatic action, and upon appropriate metrical variation of clear and vivid language. Although sometimes bombastic and melodramatic, the work reveals an auspicious talent far in advance of its author's seventeen years.

Sertorius is the actor in "The Last Banquet" as he wearily struggles to uphold the Republic while foreseeing the eventual victory of Pompey. Two former comrades of Sertorius attempt to assassinate him in a dramatic action that goes beyond anything Browning attempted—perhaps, indeed, too far for the form.

But Sertorius comes alive out of history as he brokenheartedly calls for his love Nydia, all that remains for him. In the second monologue Lucullus dines with Cicero and Pompey and wavers between a longing for the old heady sense of conquest with his legions and nostalgia for a girl he had found during the sacking of a city. Subsequent portraits reveal Crassus preparing to leave his tent to face the encircling Parthian cavalry, Cicero groaning under the burden of adjudication, and Caesar in Gaul deciding to march on Ariminium to begin the civil war. Pompey comes last, after the decisive battle of Pharsalia. The day is Caesar's, and the Republic is gone; but Pompey dreams that "'somewhere, beyond all, there still endures / That pure Republic: its white walls shine'" (47). A similar concern with the fate of the American republic and with its ideal form was to appear in much of Benét's later poetry and prose.

This first published poem by Benét also reveals his technical versatility and forceful style. The rather irregular blank verse which predominates moves with proper emphasis according to the speaker, shifting from the leisurely movement of Lucullus' lines to the brisk directness of Caesar's speech. When Cicero broods on the treacheries of life, the meter changes to rhymed couplets in dactylic heptameters, somewhat in the manner of Swinburne. Crassus in his last moments reflects that "'To praise is hard, easy to damn. / I failed in this. Some other will succeed'" (24). Then his mood changes and he recalls the Republic's greatness:

"Ere the first sword was sharpened and the first trumpet blown
  Rome looked upon the new-made lands and marked them
      for her own!
  Ere the first ship was timbered and the first rudder hung
  Rome held the oceans in her hands, splendid and stern
      and young!"

(26)

The metrical and syntactical balance and contrast in these lines make evident Benét's technical skill and his preference for pronounced rhythmical effects. His liking for vivid imagery drawn from the more familiar realms of life is demonstrated in Lucullus' lines comparing life to a platter of coins over which we exclaim. For him only one coin remains, an old Greek one sent him by Demetrius and reminiscent of the face of Lucullus' lost love. The passage borrows Byron's epithet "burning" for Greek beauty, perhaps intentionally, and the coin image lacks high originality, but it is appropriate and adds another dimension to the portrait of Lucullus because it shows his ability to conceive of his love in direct ways and to associate the coin of friendship with the remembered coin of love and beauty. The metaphor is striking and functions in two ways but does not possess the multiple meanings of much modern poetry.

Five Men and Pompey also differs from much modern poetry in that it has one of the great themes: the fate of a civilization. The poem's overall effect lies somewhere between melodrama and tragedy, and it hardly achieves greatness; but overall competence it does attain, despite youthful exuberances of meter and diction and drama. All in all, it is an astonishing achievement for a seventeen-year-old.

II "The Hemp" and Other Ballads

The two poems which followed the Roman portraits are inferior to them, particularly *The Drug-Shop; or, Endymion in Edmonstown*.[6] Although it won its author a poetry prize at Yale,[7] its chief importance is biographical. It reveals Benét's love and admiration for Keats and exemplifies again Benét's tendency to juxtapose romanticism and modern realism. In this instance he does so by placing Keats's mythological hero among the products of a twentieth-century American drugstore.

"The Hemp,"[8] written a year earlier than *The Drug-Shop*, retells in ballad form an incident drawn from early Virginia history: the story of the pirate Captain Hawk, his rape of Sir Henry's daughter, and his eventual death at the hands of the vengeful father. This lurid tale Benét transformed into appropriately stirring metrics, with beats as emphatic as a marching drum's. Full of melodramatic imagery—for example, "His name bestrode the seas like Death"—the ballad compels attention by its controlled violence of sound and incident. It deflects critical esteem through its violent but superficial extremes of characterization and by its costume clichés of plot and setting. Yet Benét almost brings it off; he almost contrives a first-rate literary ballad.

Benét comes so close to this achievement because of his sure control of rhythm, which is unfalteringly adjusted to the story's development; because of the power of his descriptions; and because of a certain philosophical element. This increment of meaning is expressed partly through symbolism and partly through a refrain which becomes progressively more ominous. The hemp which Hawk swears will never hang him is finally grown by Sir Henry, is spun and twisted, made into rope, and finally placed around the pirate's neck. In the terminal refrain, *"the hemp clings fast to a dead man's throat, / And blind fate gathers back its seeds."* However, the symbolism of fate and seeds was not to have fruitful poetic issue until *John Brown's Body.* An extended ballad, "The Hemp" loses by its failure to employ either the compression of the finer folk ballads or the understatement and subtle metrical effects of William Morris' superb "The Haystack in the Floods."

Benét returned to the ballad, ultimately with better results, in subsequent volumes of poetry: *Young Adventure* (New York, 1918); *Heavens and Earth* (New York, 1920); and *Tiger Joy* (New York, 1925). "Three Days Ride"[9] is notable for a fine refrain with steadily darkening import, but this tale of aristocratic English lovers fleeing a villainous brother and his evil band is too familiar and too reliant upon the small change of a chase to merit serious consideration. "Habberton's Plow,"[10] a ballad with an American setting, is a grim story of a father who murders his daughter's lover, just returned from the Civil War, in order to keep the soldier from obtaining a New England farm. Thirty years later the daughter, while plowing, turns up her lover's skeleton and then kills her father with the plow blade. But Benét did not think as a New Englander in writing this poem, and the story could as well have taken place on the other side of the Atlantic. Stale romantic images like "aching June" are another source of the poem's disjunction of setting and style.

In a group of ballads collected in *Tiger Joy* (the title comes from Shelley's poetic drama *Prometheus Unbound*), Benét found styles perfectly suited to very different themes: thumping rhythms and Georgia hill dialect for "The Mountain Whippoorwill";[11] swift, flailing couplets for "King David";[12] and clear, sweet pioneer music for "The Ballad of William Sycamore (1790-1880)."[13]

The first of these three poems—subtitled "A Georgia Romance" —drew on Benét's boyhood memories of that state and of North Carolina.[14] Benét said that in this poem he attempted to adapt the traditional ballad form to a contemporary American theme, to vary it as he chose, and to use colloquial speech—"get the note of the boxwood fiddle into it, if it could be done. I had heard the mountain fiddlers in the North Carolinas, and their tunes stuck in my head."[15] The result was more than a minor *tour de force* since Benét not only managed to suggest through the imagery and movement of his verse the swift country bowing, but the quality of life in the hills of Georgia and Carolina. The poem is lighted with touches of pioneer tall-tale humor and old-time religion. The narrator, winner of the Essex County Fiddlers' Show at a fair, is individualized as an imaginative orphan who conceives of his parents as a fiddle and a whippoor-will; and his initial bravado, followed by his genuine apprecia-tion for his rivals' skill and his feeling that he has lost the contest, adds drama to his victory.

Benét's ability to suggest the range, movement, and quality of the fiddling does most to make the poem. Overwhelmed by Old Dan Wheeling's playing, who "fiddled the wind by the lonesome moon / . . . fiddled a most almighty tune," the story-teller calls on his identity with the mountains where he was born as his unique resource:

> Whippoorwill, singin' thu' the mountain hush,
> Whippoorwill, shoutin' from the burnin' bush,
> Whippoorwill, cryin' in the stable-door,
> Sing tonight as yuh never sang before!

Thus inspired, he wins. The sometimes coarse and violent language of this ballad is justified on the grounds of realism; also, it is modified by the genuine folk poetry which colors the poem. Repeated references to the whippoorwill—first as the mother of the narrator, then as a nature symbol whose singing represents both the fiddler and the fiddler's genius—provide another unifying device. "The Mountain Whippoorwill" was Benét's first ballad shaped wholly from native materials by his full resources for giving them life.

Benét's "Ballad of William Sycamore," often chosen by editors of anthologies to represent his lyrical Americanism, deserves the widespread admiration accorded it by common readers and by at least some professional ones. The latter include the redoubtable F. O. Matthiessen, who was for the most part unfavorably disposed toward Benét's work but regarded this poem as notable.[16] The clarity and precision with which Benét sums up the life of a representative though idealized frontiersman are here precisely the qualities to be conveyed by the ballad meter, with its exact rhymes and beat as exciting as the frontier's "Money Musk," on which the pioneer is reared. Benét adroitly alternates iambics and dactyls and introduces just enough metrical variations in the short line to suggest a rippling song.

The clean, fresh life of the frontier is set forth in the succession of American images which move through the poem: the green fir that serves as the mother's doctor; the silver-handled ewer and bayberry candles that are boyhood memories; the snuff-brown frontiersmen with their long squirrel-rifles; the girl like a Salem clipper; and the sons sowed like apple-seed on the wagon trails. Like this last one, several of the images evoke birth or death, and the peaceful immortality of William Sycamore at the end moves the poem into the larger realm of myth. Sycamore's name, an image played upon in the image of the pine that attended his birth, suggests, of course, the evergreen symbol of immortality. His life-in-death continues in the wilderness earth from which he sprang and which he symbolizes; he is one of the innumerable sons of Natty Bumppo who fled westward from the encroaching towns. The poem which bears Sycamore's name has as intimate a relationship to the legends of the frontier which the American mind remembers. So long as the national mind does so, it will find this ballad rooted deep and strong in the country's history, and perhaps even deeper in the universal urge to be at one with nature in her wild, free beauty.

Benét's equally famed "American Names,"[17] written while he was living in Paris during the late 1920's and working on *John Brown's Body*, is an offshoot of the epic.[18] This ballad is a direct expression of Benét's love for his distant homeland, an emotion nourished rather than diminished by his temporary exile. The poem does not summon up as much history and legend as "William Sycamore," but it draws some names, crisp and tangy as Winesaps, from American history in order to press from them the flavor of our native juices. Benét's line "I am tired of loving a foreign muse" echoes Emerson's historic utterance in his "American Scholar" address of 1821: "We have listened too long to the courtly muses of Europe."

Benét descends into no chauvinism in this statement: he concedes the unique beauties of Old World names and the cultures they symbolize and merely asserts his preference for the culture of his native land. Indeed, judged by traditional aesthetic criteria, Europe's names are more beautiful. Seine and Piave, the poet calls "silver spoons," and the names of some English counties are like "hunting tunes." Rue des Martyrs and Bleeding-Heart-Yard guard "a magic ghost." Yet the poet longs for American places, Yankee ships and Yankee dates, even for the preposterously comic Skunktown Plain; he yearns for a newer ghost. Henry and John—presumably Longfellow and Whittier—were not thus, but the poet wonders if they never watched for Nantucket light "after the tea and the laurels had stood all night." Here Benét associates the nineteenth-century New England poets with the borrowed English and classical culture which they represented.

"American Names" demonstrates the same sensitive control of meter that characterizes "William Sycamore," as well as the same command of imagery, although much of the poem's effect comes from the connotations of proper names strategically placed.[19] The fourth stanza uses the objectionable term "blue-gum nigger," but Benét identifies him honorably as the singer of blues, the American music. A Salem tree (a majestic chestnut), a Santa Cruz rawhide quirt, and a bottle of Boston sea complete this list of American symbols. Each is recognizably American but not banal as an image: a lesser poet might have longed for Coney Island or a five-gallon Stetson. The poem's movement and meaning gather rising emphasis in the final stanza, with its succession of short, simple sentences and its assertion of a love returning home triumphant over the body's alien burial. Benét's final prayer that his heart be buried at Wounded Knee gives the poem deeper significance than it has hitherto possessed, since this South Dakota town was the scene of a tragic Indian massacre by the Seventh Cavalry in the final clash between Indians and government troops.[20] The poet thus identifies himself inextricably with the mixture of good and bad that is his country, and his choice of burial place implies a desire for national atonement and peace.

"King David" proved Benét's ability to employ the ballad for a non-American and more sophisticated purpose, although the poem undoubtedly has American religious implications. A scathingly satiric retelling of the biblical story of David, Uriah, and Bathsheba, it points up David's smug egotism and facile repentance of his sins. Benét's edged phrasing underscores criticism of the Old Testament concept of a God who is a jealous God, a crafty God, and a too-forgiving God; and he embellishes the story as told in II Samuel so as to emphasize David's lustfulness, deviousness, and pride. The broad ironies of the story emerge through Benét's trenchant characterizations and through stinging heroic couplets with their snapping terminal iambics. The sly insertions of the refrain—"The Lord God is a jealous God"—and its variations emphasize the mocking attitude of the poet in his guise as a devout contemporary chronicler. Benét masterfully combines striking, sensuous Hebrew metaphor —Bathsheba's body glimmers like the flesh of aloes in candlelight—with his own ironic imagery and vivid phrasing, to make "King David" a poem that fastens on the memory.

The six parts and two-hundred-odd lines of "King David" culminate with a triumphantly sardonic description of David's seven nights of repentance which end with the death of his and Bathsheba's child and with David's solacing of her out of his great contentment. She, being woman merely, grieves for a while, permits herself to be soothed, and conceives again. The name of this second child is Solomon (Benét puts the name in boldface), who is God's staff until the end of his days. Solomon's wisdom Benét slyly does not mention, but the reader may recall it as a criterion for the follies of David and, even more fundamentally, the absurdity of those who believe in a deity so debased by human characteristics as to smite hard the heathen and exalt such a ready sinner and successful supplicator as David.

The distinctions of this irreverent ballad won for it the coveted poetry award of *The Nation* for 1922, but it brought the editors of that eminent liberal journal a heavy influx of indignant letters objecting to Benét's supposed immorality and blasphemy. But although "King David" can be associated with the juvenile pseudo-diabolism of Benét's novel *The Beginning of Wisdom* (1921), with the skepticism reflected in *Jean Huguenot* (1923), another novel, and with his notable short poem "For All Blasphemers,"[21] it should not be taken as a full statement of his religious position. In his letters Benét refers to himself as an agnostic,[22] and his poem "Hands"[23] is deeply reverent. While

"King David" offended many conventional or orthodox believers, it can be defended as moral in the sense that it challenges an uncritical acceptance of an Old Testament story. A religious ethic which praises a Deity harsh toward unbelievers while indulgent toward devout sinners, no matter how deliberately sinful and shallowly repentant, is a less consistently lofty system than its advocates prefer to believe. But whatever the reaction to the religious content of the poem, there is no denying its superb style and structure.

III *Of Youth and Of Love*

The large majority of Benét's early poems are undistinguished by any exacting standard, ideological or aesthetic, and they particularly contrast with his handful of fine ballads. The title of *Young Adventure* indicates a group of poems dealing with some aspect of the American youth that continued to be one of Benét's major concerns, both as subject and audience. Portraits of a baby, of a boy, and of young love[24] succeed in plausibly presenting infantile, boyish, and youthful psychology, but in the romantically strained accents of Benét's least attractive style. "Young Blood"[25] is stuffed with clichés and is garishly dependent on the shock of revelation—in this instance, as sustained by a victim of a bachelor party on the eve of his wedding who finds himself in bed the next morning with a sleazy prostitute. "The General Public"[26] takes its epigraph from Browning's fine poem on Shelley and then proceeds to shatter the reader's memory of the Victorian's well-sustained tone of wonder and understated climax with an overwrought, melodramatic picture of a persecuted Shelley with flame-like eyes. These and similar poems of Benét's can safely be consigned to their respective realms of the commonplace and the sensational.

Among the mass of Benét's minor poems gleam occasional diamond-like lyrics and some excellent light verse, including humorous poems and some fancies and bouquets for his lady. The "Hands" in the previously mentioned poem of this title belong to his wife, his brother, and to Benét himself. The delicate hands of his wife and the cultivated hands of his brother are contrasted with Benét's "children of affront, / Base mechanics at the most / That have sometimes touched a ghost." The poet asks a blessing upon the first four hands but for his own hands prays for an iron stake for them to attempt to break. The powerful first lines of the last stanza invoke the blessings of "God the Son and God the Sire / And God the triple-handed fire" in a magnificent metaphorical linking of the Trinity with the human objects of the poet's invocation. Benét asks finally only a blessing for "four hands of courtesy," and his humility is the proper attitude to precede the "Amen." The short hymn-like lines, liturgically emphatic rhythm, and rich though compact imagery of this lyric combine to give it a power out of proportion to its length.

Compression also characterizes Benét's next best short lyric, "Memory,"[27] though its intensity is uneven, heightening through the second of the two eight-line stanzas, after the more open statement of the first. Its poignancy comes from its seizing of the essences of life—love, birth, age, wisdom, death—and contrasting them in terse, unrhymed lines built with monosyllables, six to eight per line. His love was the best part of his life, the poet says; death does not matter, for life is a ghost in the flesh that comes and goes. With an almost choking ellipsis, the poet acknowledges that though the moon burns lamp-bright it will not have *that* brightness. . . . He said her name sleeping and waking. The underlying emotion—tragic awareness of the inevitable loss of life's dearest possession—surges through the silence of what is unsaid.

A delightful cluster of gay and fanciful tributes to his sweetheart (*Selected Works*, I, 353-62), whom he later married, tributes airy and delicate as a handful of silver milkweed spores on summer wind, includes the lovely "To Rosemary" (353-54). In it, her essence is as old music boxes, young tawny kittens, wild-strawberry seed, and something indefinable, fire in crystal. "Nomenclature" (354) is still finer, with its impressionistic descriptions of the qualities of names (some people have names "full of sizzling esses like a family quarrel of snakes") and its subtle appreciations of the lady's qualities, culminating in an ecstatic rush of words and images. Charming enough to turn any lady's head, although they are styled for Benét's lady, are "Difference" (355), contrasting the wilderness map of his mind with her lovely and delicate psyche; "To Rosemary, on the Methods by Which She Might Become an Angel" (357), playfully prophesying the impudent nature of her immortality; and "Dulce Ridentem" (361), lightly celebrating his youth and her "moth-wing soul." "Nonsense Song" (356) weaves in a deft tribute to Rosemary, along with the fooling. "In a Glass of Water Before Retiring" (358-59) is as drowsily sweet music as a lady could wish, while the companion poem "Evening and Morning" (357-58) imaginatively traces the course of her sleep until break of day.

Several poems lying somewhere between the pathos of "Memory" and the playful gallantries of the fanciful poems complete the limited emotional spectrum of Benét's love poetry. The limitations arose simply from the sustained happiness of his courtship of a fine and charming woman and their marriage of more than twenty years, which was terminated only by Benét's death.[28] Throughout their long relationship Benét wrote poems to her, all of them testifying to the steadfastness of his affection. "All Night Long"[29] tells of the poet's vigil over the serene sleep of his beloved and of her awaking into the beautiful day. Their passion is indirectly suggested by an image of the rising morning; Benét is no anatomist of love. "With a Gift of Silver Candlesticks"[30] symbolically bestows one lovely gift for his wife's body, one for her spirit. The giving is a gesture gravely worshipful. Benét's love for his wife as expressed in his poems to her was deep and sensitive, wholly admirable; it was based on keen admiration for her loyalty, gaiety, wit, imagination, and highly individual beauty.

IV *A Book of Americans*

United also by mutual love of their native land, the Benéts collaborated in writing a clever series of verse biographies, *A Book of Americans* (1933). Benét conceived of the project in 1933 after seeing an exhibition of children's books,[31] and his and his wife's dedication of the book to their three children—"our other works in collaboration"—indicates the audience they wrote it for. Benét's lifelong interest in American youth found expression in verse portraits which sprang from the same creative impulse that, fusing humor and history, produced the Daniel Webster tales.

A Book of Americans consists of fifty-odd short poems about famous and infamous figures in American history; they range from Christopher Columbus to Woodrow Wilson and include such national villains as Aaron Burr. Mrs. Benét contributed the portraits of the five women—Pocahantas, Abigail Adams, Dolly Madison, Nancy Hanks, and Clara Barton—while her husband sketched the men, and described clipper ships, Negro spirituals, and some other unique products of the American imagination. A few collective portraits—notably of the Puritans and Pilgrims— are also provided. The result of the collaboration is a winning little book with the twin appeals of humor and insight, both historical and biographical, for adults not too stodgy to enjoy occasional quiet fun at the expense of some national heroes. (Wilson, Benét observes, eschewed his boyhood name of Tommy for his resounding public name.)

That vast and mysterious audience called "juvenile" doubtless includes many who would enjoy the nursery-rhyme meter, the clear, short rhymes, and the general freshness spiced with diverting surprises that the Benéts tucked into *A Book of Americans*. Ulysses S. Grant, the youthful reader will learn, was a great soldier and gentleman but a poor president, though an honest one. The poet, pondering the contradictions of human nature, reaches into his lexicon for a Scottish dialect word and concludes that men are "kittle cattle." But, he asks, "How many rhymers, children dear, / Have ever won a battle?" The point is made so sweetly that it should go down easily, though *kittle* and a few other grown-up words may bring calls for grown-up help.

Judicious praise and blame for the men and women portrayed are what the book's "Apology" asks of the reader, whether young or old; and the Benéts themselves observe the dictates of justice. Sometimes, however, there is nothing to laud, as with Daniel Drew, the nineteenth-century financial wizard, a "sanctimonious old sneak" whose death the poet terms fortunate, since it pre- vented Drew from further stealing. If the reader wonders why the poet dug up this tarnished scamp from history's refuse, the answer is that there were more men like Daniel Drew, and there still are. Obviously no one will question the presence of Crawford Long and William Morton, the little-known doctor and dentist who, working separately, discovered the anesthetic properties of ether and thus made possible painless surgery. Earnest patriots, however, may object to such generosity of spirit as Benét shows in reminding the reader that, although the triumph of Oliver De Lancey, the Tory—or Loyalist—general would have meant no Stars and Stripes, there are two sides to every question. Idolators of the Puritans and Pilgrims will resent Benét's observation that every time we think we are better than someone else and that he must do as we say or we'll whack him, the Puritan is still in our backyard. Fanatical anti-Puritans will criticize Benét's concluding emphasis on the Puritans' resolute courage, their never asking to fight with less than giants. *A Book of Americans* is marked by a largeness of vision and a tolerance characteristic of American liberalism at its best; it recognizes that our nation was built by many individuals and groups with varying mixtures of good and bad traits.

V *Gothic Themes*

That broad romantic hope of Benét's which was stirred by the American Dream contrasts strikingly with the midnight aspect of his romanticism. Sometimes, indeed, his sense of the macabre explored some frailty or sickness in the national soul, but it also had a more personal aspect. Several lyrics of medium emotional weight reveal the darker reaches of his mind, his rebelliousness, or his intermittent preoccupation with such Gothic themes as death or insanity.

"Architects"[32] follows the pattern of "Hands" in that it sets up distinctions between several persons close to the poet by means of a symbolic extension of identifying traits, but it expresses only the bleakest kind of faith. Benét contrasts his son's fortress of pride, his daughter's shield of wit, his wife's coffin of lead wrought from "counterfeit tears of mourners" in which she rests with the blessed calm of a long-dead saint, and the poet's own arid, craftily dug grave. It will not last till Judgment Day, he concedes, but it will not cripple him either; and though some may think it confining, when he enters it he can keep the "nakedness of an arrow." This somewhat obscure poem seems to restate Benét's stoic view of death, a conception relieved only by a wreath of poetry. "Architects" is Benét's closest approach to a modernist metaphysical poem: its five conventional quatrains enclose an involved structure packed with mortal ironies.

Irony wrenched into the grotesque is the pattern of "Ghosts of a Lunatic Asylum,"[33] which attempts to heighten the terrors of insanity by describing an abandoned institution haunted by the shades of the former inmates. Benét treats the theme superficially, however, and the effect lessens rather than accentuates the horror. Considerably more powerful is "Minor Litany,"[34] which makes use of a traditional Christian liturgical form to achieve a mordant irony. In a time of confusion, "with few clear stars," either public or private, the poet supplicates on behalf of those he calls the lost, the half-lost, and the desperate—in current terminology, the mentally ill. The cumulative effect of Benét's precisely stated—or understated—dictionary of types in need of, or already under the care of, psychiatrists is almost unbearably depressing. The poet calls first upon Christ for mercy, then upon Freud, then upon Life; and a later invocation near the end of the poem implores only the mercy of drugs. The final stanzas drive home the widespread and relentless incidence of psychic traumas and climax the rising note of hopelessness—the poor in mental health ye have always with ye, so to speak—inherent in a litany without God. The ending carelessly dissipates something of the carefully built-up mood by its half-facetious phrasing, and the total meaning is circumscribed by its descriptive and unanalytical approach; yet the poem is disturbing.

VI *Burning City*

The cream of Benét's poems thus far examined consists of his four fine ballads, three of them American flavored, of two exquisite lyrics, of a cluster of love poems, and of *A Book of Americans*. The ballads have an arresting originality of style and content; the love poems have a charming music Benét's own, and, in a sense, his wife's. *A Book of Americans* teaches and delights with an effectiveness out of proportion to its slightness. Yet in their totality these poems can lay claim to no more than a modest place in twentieth-century American poetry, nor did Benét claim more for them. In several ways—his general preference for traditional form, his unabashed love of his country, his somewhat ambiguous religious skepticism, his avoidance of complex symbolism and of distillations of themes remote from the commonalty of American experience—his poetry was vulnerable to attack on the critical battlegrounds of the 1920's and 1930's. The American themes were anathema to both Marxists and expatriates. The Metaphysical critics could find no elaborate interweavings of "wit"; and the whole center of this movement around T. S. Eliot was rooted in an implicit cultural, social, political, and religious anti-Americanism. Back of Eliot lay a significant tradition of cultural alienation stretching back to Nathaniel Hawthorne and crowned by Henry James. This tradition had, and has, numerous and well-entrenched supporters, particularly in the academic world.

A detailed examination of these points of view as they bear upon Benét's poetry is neither feasible nor necessary in this study. In a broad sense, America's growing political maturity and cultural resources, particularly in literature, have provided the answers to those who have held that an American literature in any way affirmative and rich was impossible of achievement. Marxist criticism offers for liberal critics a single viable insight: that class conflicts exist in life and may be reflected in literature. Metaphysical criticism has provided innumerable insights into individual works of literature and has been instrumental in shattering nineteenth-century literary traditions, a valuable accomplishment, on the whole. Narrowness and dogmatism have often attended this school, however. At any rate, its point of view is, I believe, adequately represented by the critic whose scrutiny of a volume of Benét's poetry I shall consider in detail.

Some criticism of Benét's poetry which may not be easily disposed of came from an avant-garde position during the 1930's. A later academic spokesman for this group was the distinguished F. O. Matthiessen, author of *American Renaissance* (1941), one of the finest scholarly and critical works of the twentieth century. Matthiessen, in his essay on modern American poetry in the definitive *Literary History of the United States* (II, 1350-51), commented that "Benét's talents have not been considered as of anything like the first order by many other poets. . . ." The page which Matthiessen devoted to Benét in his survey left no room for critical analysis, though it is reasonable to suppose that many graduate students and professors have accepted the short essay as highly authoritative.

Earlier, another influential critic, in an extended attack from advanced positions held by the aesthetic (though not political) left, made clear in trenchant detail his reasons for disliking Benét. Morton Dauwen Zabel, editor of *Poetry* and a fine critic, in a review of Benét's *Burning City* (New York, 1936) in that important magazine, charged that Benét was the latest representative in a long line of American poets, going back to Longfellow and Bryant, whom Zabel labels the "bardic romantics."[35] The whole tradition, according to Zabel, has been "hostile to eccentric talent or refined taste, scornful of modernity or exotic influence. . . ."

Zabel seizes on *Burning City* because it enables him to illustrate the distinction he wishes to make between a bard and a poet. The former, as exemplified by Benét, is, among other things, indiscriminating in both subject matter and style. Zabel asserts that although Benét discusses social and moral degeneration, he does not grasp their significance with either his sensibilities or his intelligence. Zabel concludes his general indictment with what amounts to critical banishment: Benét writes "passable verse journalism." Along with Benét, Zabel consigns to oblivion *The New Yorker,* which was publishing some of Benét's poetry, including "Notes To Be Left in a Cornerstone," one of the longer poems in *Burning City.* Also damned are Paul Engle, the poet-professor whom Zabel regards as Benét's model, and H. G. Wells and Conan Doyle, the supposed progenitors of Benét's poems about the future. Zabel, spokesman for high art and the devoted seekers and practitioners of it and editor of the single most important American outlet for the new poetry, is intent on attacking not only the lower levels of popular literature but the more sophisticated upper strata of it occupied by *The New Yorker* and by certain academic circles.

Zabel carries on his attack against Benét through a scrutiny of "Ode to Walt Whitman" as the most ambitious poem in *Burning City.* After a severe though not injudicious analysis, Zabel concludes that the poem, despite some merits, is essentially derivative, uninspired, and obvious in meaning and technique. Since the basic issue raised by Zabel—the conflict between popular and élite art in a democracy—is a perennial one, and since his criticism of Benét as bard offers a fruitful means of appraising Benét's minor poetry, a point-by-point consideration of Zabel's analysis of the "Ode" is warranted.

Zabel begins by conceding that the first section of the ode is written in Benét's "most charming manner," a relative degree of praise that would be evasive were it not followed by the assertion that Benét's free verse catches Whitman's spirit very successfully, notably in the image of giant, approaching footsteps. The spatial limitations of Zabel's essay prevent him from spelling out the details of Benét's achievement here. Partly they reside in the fact that the footsteps symbolize not only the death that walks through *Leaves of Grass* but also suggest Walt himself in his marches across America as seer and prophet. They further suggest the personal identification with death that marks some of Whitman's poems, such as "When Lilacs Last in the Dooryard Bloom'd." Technically Benét's line in this section resembles Whitman's without duplicating it (in so far as Whitman's diversified free metrics could be paralleled). In its general movement, however, through the accumulation of reiterated facts and participial phrases, Benét's verse is finely evocative of Whitman's.

Notable also in this first section are Benét's imagery and phrasing. Drawn from the same native sources as Whitman's, they are similarly clear and concrete, or symbolically ambiguous. A picture of Death as "half-seen through the wet, sweet sea-fog of youth" awakens the surging echoes of Whitman's "Out of the Cradle Endlessly Rocking," his entangled childhood reminiscence of some crucial experience of death on Long Island. The lines which Benét gives Whitman to speak appropriately set off the calamus—generative symbol of a group of poems in *Leaves of Grass*—against nightbane, symbol of death and also of the night of "Out of the Cradle," in which the boy gains his knowledge of the universality of death and life. This sort of skillful alluding to Whitman's poetry is akin to borrowing, in respect to originality; but Benét also provides a fresh and noble American image which is characteristic of Whitman but does not occur in *Leaves of Grass*. This is a simile which likens Whitman to one of the great old herd-leaders among the buffalo, innocent, curly-browed, with "kingly eyes," who die on the plains and have their tongues cut out by hunters. The image is physically and symbolically apt, descriptive of Whitman in body, character, and final end. Not all of the imagery is so fine, but on the whole Zabel somewhat underrates the value of this section of the "Ode," though he finally calls it "impressive."

In the second section of the poem Zabel notes a falling-off from the initial excellence because of repetition and direct exposition. He also declares that this part "betrays the absence of a central conception of Whitman as the dialogue between the poet and his interrogator descends to the most obvious contrasts between Whitman's dream of democracy and its present frustration. . . ." Zabel is correct in perceiving a general poetic decline in this section, although in only one or two instances is the imagery banal, as in "women with dry breasts." Some of it is on nearly as high a level as that in the first section; there is, for example, "bridges arched like the necks of beautiful horses," a simile which establishes a beautiful parallel between the modern industrial world and the animal world which Whitman loved. Again, to suggest the active principle of evil at work in the Depression, Benét fashions the powerfully repellent image of tentworms shrouding the trees of America. On the other hand, some of the exposition is flat and sacrifices the concentration and multiple suggestiveness of the tentworm metaphor. Lines such as " 'We have made many, fine new toys' " and " 'There is a rust on the land' " lie somewhere between the banal and the merely uninspired, and they partially bear out Zabel's charge.

Zabel's complaint that Benét engages in repetition is, however, unsupported, unless he means that there is some dilution of the theme of a land blighted by waste, injustice, and folly. Certainly the main elements causing the Depression require description, and this Benét provides, though not from the best of his imaginative resources. Zabel's assertion that Benét lacks a central conception of Whitman is equally unexplained; indeed, it is puzzling since in this section Benét sets forth his ideas about the causes and nature of the Depression, in answer to Whitman's questions as the latter rests on a hillside in his life-in-death. Benét's description reveals the compassion for the ill-clothed, ill-housed, and ill-fed and the anger over economic and social injustice that liberals felt during the Depression. This section is admittedly inferior to the first one, but its basic structure is surely inevitable. The alternative—to have Whitman make pronouncements about the Depression, to make him the principal spokesman in the section—would demand a conception of him as omnipresent and omniscient. Benét's method—to have him ask questions concerning his native land after having been wakened by his modern lovers—permits the tragedy of Whitman's final query: Was the blood of the Civil War spilt for nothing?

In the short third section, with its two- and three-beat lines and quiet intensity, Benét provides metrical and emotional relief from the extended gravities of the preceding section. A lone man, presumably a poet, who comes to seek the arbutus, a symbol of renewal connected with both the grass and the calamus symbols of Whitman, signifies reaffirmation of the American spirit and identification with the soil. Love and courage motivate the symbolic action. Zabel approves of the style of this passage and of the delicacy of some of its images, but he says of the latter that they are strung out and involved to poor effect. The section as a whole, Zabel believes, does not strengthen the formal unity of the poem. Unquestionably, however, the human and natural symbols in the section establish vital connections with Whitman. They also forecast the rising note of national affirmation which dominates the fourth and final section. Zabel's objection to the unharmonious structural role of this section is not valid. Moreover, Benét limits his images to an uncomplicated handful, though they are not taken from his freshest stock of native metaphor.

With Zabel's strictures on the opening passage of the fourth part of the ode, one may readily agree: Benét does lapse into "slovenly sarcasm" on the world's way with poets. His tone descends to the colloquial and the exasperated, and it is hardly saved by a succession of one-line descriptions of the terrible demises of poets other than Whitman. The remaining three-fourths of the section consist of a panoramic vision of America in the Whitman manner, slightly modified by Benét's quickness of perception, and finally centering on the Mississippi as the nation's great artery. Zabel acknowledges Benét's usual skill in catching here the texture of American life, but he damns this portion as a familiar checklist of Benét's usual references and says that it invites a dangerous comparison with the handling of the same theme by a true poet, Hart Crane. Zabel's vehemence is unwarranted, and his feeling that he has heard all this before remains unsubstantiated. Benét's conclusion for his ode nevertheless remains disappointing because of its obvious technique; superficially complimentary to Whitman, Benét neglects Whitman's preference for originality rather than convention.

My critical analysis of the "Ode to Walt Whitman" is thus in general agreement with Zabel's, although it parts company at several points concerning imagery, structure, and conception. Moreover, Zabel's initial insistence on Benét's lifelong ambition to become a bard in the genteel tradition is unfounded and illogical; it is difficult to reconcile Benét's admiration for Whitman—anathema to conservatives—with Zabel's charge.

Zabel consigns not only the tribute to Whitman but all the other more important poems in *Burning City* to the same critical trash heap of the commonplace. He singles out "Litany for Dictatorships" (12-16) and "Ode to the Austrian Socialists" (17-21) as examples of tedious cataloguing and banal thinking. The three nightmares—"Metropolitan Nightmare" (69-72), "Nightmare, with Angels" (73-75), and "Nightmare Number Three" (76-79)—Zabel castigates as juvenile in conception and vulgar in style, although he implies that they convey some sense of impending catastrophe. "Metropolitan Nightmare" and "Nightmare Number Three" merit some attention since they have been included in several anthologies and exemplify Benét in his role as prophet. These poems were followed in 1940 by a group which includes "Nightmare for Future Reference" (36) and "Nightmare at Noon" (37). To these should be added "Notes To Be Left in a Cornerstone"(3-9), the best of the longer poems in *Burning City*, although Zabel does not mention it.

All of these poems are warnings of doom for America as represented by New York City. The forms of the catastrophe envisioned include destruction by natural causes, annihilation through war or through universal sterility brought on by war, and ruin of an unspecified sort brought on by collective madness for money or some other general folly or failure. The time is the present, the near future, or World War III; and the speaker or narrator is the poet or, in "Nightmare Number Three," an average man. The style is prevailingly conversational, with only an occasional rise to a more lyrical line; and since the symbolism is easily grasped, these poems for the most part communicate their meaning with little effort on the part of the reader. The group is full of vivid descriptive detail organized for maximum effect. In two of the poems full revelation of the fateful circumstances comes in the last line. In "Metropolitan Nightmare" a termite found carrying in its jaw a bright crumb of steel brings realization of the terrible adaptation of the insects to a city of skyscrapers which they have invaded as a result of a change in the Gulf Stream. In "Nightmare for Future Reference"—an ironic title—an account of World War III and its sudden cessation when women revolt withholds until the last line the fact that the race can no longer reproduce itself.

The situation in these poems is unfolded with Benét's usual facility, and now and then an increment of meaning is furnished by indirection. "Metropolitan Nightmare" gains through the unstressed import of the indifference of New Yorkers to the silent peril come upon them, an attitude suggestive of a casualness about real though unstated dangers. Mostly, however, Benét makes his meaning explicit, sometimes to the point of overstatement; and in general these poems are superficial and contrived to produce sensational effects. "Nightmare at Noon" is more thoughtful than the others and is within the realm of reality, but its style never achieves any more distinction than a conversational irony or unechoing plainness.

"Nightmare Number Three," the best of the group except for "Notes To Be Left in a Cornerstone," is a nondramatic monologue in which the speaker describes himself and his situation without attaining any insight into either. In his account of a revolt of the machines against their modern American masters, the hopelessly trapped fellow consoles himself with the thought of the gratitude his Plymouth must have for the swell French horn he gave it. Foolish senators, Wall Street brokers, and petty uses for the power of machines are manifestations of the enslavement of man by his creations. Now the machines have learned to think, while their creators have stopped thinking. Imaginative details such as the octopus-tendrils of a telephone switchboard waving over the head of a strangled business executive make the poem arresting, though its ultimate quality is garish melodrama.

The mood and style of "Notes To Be Left in a Cornerstone" are quiet; yet they come close to creating an overwhelming sense of the tragedy in the fall of a great city. The cause of the disaster is hinted at only; Benét is unconcerned with the means of destruction. What absorbs him is the quality of life in New York, its variety and contradictions, its seasonal extremes, its ugliness and beauty. Benét conveys precisely and vividly the terrible heat of summer, the long cold of winter and its hushes broken only by the scritch-scratch of shovels, the sharp stimuli of fall, the short loveliness of spring, with the new moon over the gray water at the end of streets. Since all this has passed away, the poem is movingly elegiac. A dignified line, often pacing several feet beyond the limits of blank verse, bears securely the elegiac mood. Some lines are notable, as when the poet laments that maps and models can never represent the city as it was:

> They cannot restore that beauty, rapid and harsh,
> That loneliness, that passion or that name.

The next to last section of the poem falters a bit as Benét, in the manner of T. S. Eliot, introduces quasi-humorous names to indicate those New Yorkers who have gone with the city; but the final section rises again to poignancy and tragic resignation.

In this poem Benét demonstrates a sensibility, a range of perception and feeling, and a sensitive and powerful style that go beyond the best of his ballads, dramatic monologues, and lyrics. Although these combined powers are not reflected elsewhere in *Burning City,* they are in this poem the manifestation of the much greater talent that had earlier produced *John Brown's Body.* Any critical estimate of Benét as a poet must be based primarily on this epic.

CHAPTER 2

The Epic:
John Brown's Body

*J*OHN BROWN'S BODY[1] is the work which first brought
Benét national fame; it is the work by which he is still best
known; and it is the work which should do the most to ensure his
permanency in the history of American literature. Spanning
five of the most crucial years in American history—from the raid
on Harper's Ferry to Lee's surrender at Appomattox Courthouse
—and memorably presenting such figures as Lincoln, Jefferson
Davis, Lee, Grant, and Stonewall Jackson, in addition to the
avenging Kansas farmer whose spirit marched for the North,
Benét's work was the boldest attempt in our literature to treat
our history poetically. Benét's imagination created a score of
characters whose fates reflect his interpretation of the human
complexities of the Civil War, and his poetic gifts enabled him
to maintain a generally high level of stylistic and narrative
achievement. The scope, structure, and style of the poem,
nearly fifteen thousand lines in length, make it, broadly speaking,
an epic in the classical sense, but it is an epic with uniquely
American qualities and themes. If *John Brown's Body* is not
quite the equal of the *Iliad* or the *Aeneid,* it was at its publication in 1928 decisively the closest approach to Homer and Vergil
that an American poet had ever made, and it still retains
this distinction. It deserves, however, to be considered on its
own merits.

I *American Heritage*

The genesis of *John Brown's Body* lay in Benét's lifelong
attachment to his native land, in his mature awareness of its
heritage of greatness and its need for literary interpretations
of that heritage. Paradoxical as it may seem at first, Benét wrote
the poem in Paris during the 1920's, a time when the city was

a Gallic Parnassus for many American writers and intellectuals, including Ernest Hemingway and F. Scott Fitzgerald. For most of these representatives of the Lost Generation, it was a period of disillusion, much of it disillusion with America. Benét liked Paris as well as the voluntary exiles did and was on friendly terms with such members of the American *avant-garde* as Archibald MacLeish and John Peale Bishop; but unlike most of them, he found that separation merely deepened his love for his country.[2] He himself was writing in Paris because he could do so more cheaply than at home. Although few of the expatriates who knew of Benét's project were enthusiastic about it, his feeling for America continued to generate his writing. He hoped that the book would have in it "'some of the landscapes, sights, the sounds of the people which are American. I am tired, not of criticism of America, for no country can be healthy without criticism, but of the small railers, conventional rebels. We also have a heritage—and not all of it wooden money.'"[3]

The nature of Benét's dedication to his poetic and patriotic task is beautifully set forth in the Invocation which precedes *John Brown's Body.* In the classical tradition revived by English poets during the Renaissance and the eighteenth century, Benét calls upon his Muse, the American Muse, for inspiration. Awed by the magnitude of his purpose, he does so with moving humility. The Muse becomes a personification of America: strong, diverse, far-flung, its essence elusive and difficult to understand. American culture is dual in nature, both European and indigenous: "As native as the shape of Navajo quivers, / And native, too, as the sea-voyaged rose." The Invocation epitomizes American history, with its record of breaking out of the English and French molds briefly forced upon the New World. Modern industrial America is still more difficult to comprehend than the America of the explorers and colonists; never do we seem to be able to distill the meaning of "the pure elixir, the American thing." But the poet recalls three cherished moments when he seemed to encounter, with an almost mystical ecstasy, the essence of America. A daylong snowfall in an Eastern town followed by a blue-shadowed night; a heat-blasted day in an industrial city; a windy day on a poppy-crowded hill—these were instants of transcendental insight when Benét caught glimpses of the Muse. From these and his other visions of America he will shape his epic.

Benét concedes that his aim may seem futile to those wise men who hold that art has no nationality, that the world of art is a world of its own. Yet he cannot resist the lure of pursuit of the American Muse, whatever the risk; although "Art has no nations," mortal men exist in nations which have their immortal moments. Benét is American born and American bred, and he will

> . . . strive at last, against an alien proof
> And by the changes of an alien moon,
> To build again that blue, American roof
> Over a half-forgotten battle-tune
> And call unsurely, from a haunted ground,
> Armies of shadows and the shadow-sound.

The Muse has a Long House (an Indian council-house) with an attic full of dead literary works which she occasionally visits, though she is indifferent to these tributes. Benét offers her only a "cup of silver air" but asks her to accept it. This product of his craftsmanship he describes as inflated in conception, inadequate in expression, clumsily contrived, generated by hot but sterile emotion. But should the Muse reward his gift with one touch of true American inspiration, then his work will glow. If the Muse does not deign to honor the work, then its failures may still serve to guide the great writers who will come after Benét.

II A *Cyclorama*

Just as this Invocation is traditional in function and form while distinctively American in imagery and tone, so is the epic as a whole classical in its structure and aim but New World in its symbolism and style. Even the classical structure is considerably modified, however: instead of the twelve tightly linked books of the *Iliad* there are eight loosely woven books. What Benét sought was, he said, the structural fluidity of a musical composition, with its loose form.[4] In the poem itself he describes it as a "cyclorama" (311), a series of large pictures placed on the wall of a circular room so as to appear in natural perspective to an observer standing in the center. But Benét describes his cyclorama as having

> . . . not the shape of the world
> Nor even the shape of this war from first to last,

> But like a totem carved, like a totem stained
> With certain beasts and skies and faces of men
> That would not let me be too quiet at night
> Till they were figured.

This is, of course, an impressionistic description of the form of the poem; Benét is disclaiming any attempt at fullness of treatment of the Civil War. In point of fact, *John Brown's Body* is closer in shape to the twelve-span bridge which may be said to be the *Iliad* than it is to a totem pole. Perhaps, however, a national railroad line with various branch lines is a more accurate metaphor for Benét's epic. It is, at any rate, unified in various ways.

John Brown himself serves as the first integrating element in the poem. His prayer to God to make him a weapon against slavery, the raid at Harper's Ferry and its effect on public opinion, and the trial and execution of Brown take up most of Book I. A "Refrain" for Brown at the end of Book IV and section four in Book V ("John Brown's soul begins to march") further develop Brown's historical significance. The final section of the epic, "the soul rests," sums up the meaning of Brown and his raid, states their present-day consequences for the United States, and derives a lesson from Brown's character and actions.

A second major unifying element in the poem consists of invented characters who represent the main regional divisions of the country. Jack Ellyat is a Connecticut boy who enlists in the Union Army; he has a Southern counterpart, Clay Wingate, of Wingate Hall, Georgia. Melora Vilas, whom Ellyat eventually marries, and her father represent the Border States and the West. Sally Dupré is the neighbor girl whom Wingate marries at the end of the war. A number of minor figures are also more or less typified by region and class. Among these are Luke Breckinridge, the feuding Tennessee mountaineer; Spade, a runaway slave; Cudjo, the Wingates' loyal slave; Lucy Weatherby, a Southern coquette; Jake Diefer, a stolid Pennsylvania farmer; and Shippey, a Northern spy. Most of the fates of these characters, major and minor, are resolved by the war.

Further important unifying elements of *John Brown's Body* are provided by symbolism and by consistent and purposeful variations in style and meter. Analysis of these elements should, however, be deferred until the historical and philosophical meanings of the epic have been considered.

III *Historical, Philosophical Significance, and Imagery*

The significance of the Civil War itself is implied or expressed in various ways throughout the poem. Benét in his Foreword says that the conflict ". . . decided how we were going to live as a nation—whether we were going to live as two nations or as one—and all the America we know is built upon that decision. If we had decided to live as two nations instead of as one, our own daily lives would be very different" (xxxiii). This simple understatement points obliquely to Benét's moderate Northern view of the Civil War; it is the moderation of Lincoln, of Whitman, and of Sandburg, the moderation that wisely and patiently sought to sustain the Union against both the Southern fanatics who would have destroyed it through rebellion and the Northern fanatics who would have sacrificed it to the end of abolishing slavery and punishing the South at whatever cost. Although Benét does not evade final judgments of men and issues, he is judicious in arriving at them, careful to follow an account of the misery and degradation of Northern prisoners of war at Andersonville with an account of the senseless shooting of Confederate prisoners in the Union camp at Newport News. When Benét writes the following, the generalization applies to both sides:

> Some men wish evil and accomplish it
> But most men, when they work in that machine
> Just let it happen somewhere in the wheels.
> The fault is no decisive villainous knife
> But the dull saw that is the routine mind.
>
> (230)

An initial key to Benét's position on the vital issues of the war—a position which is fully revealed only after the unlocking of several doors—is provided in the prelude, "The Slaver." Mainly a dialogue between the Yankee captain of a slave ship and his young mate who is on his first voyage in the trade, the prelude emphasizes the economic motive lying behind slavery. It also skillfully implicates both sides in responsibility for the institution. The ship's cargo is destined for the South, but the New England

slave trader quotes from his Bible to justify the transaction as
"'spreading the Lord's seed.'" The mate's nausea after going
into the hold and his foreboding about the consequences of
slavery suggest the North's divided conscience and partial guilt.

Benét's conception of the causes of the Civil War is no single-
minded economic determinism. Half a dozen considerations make
this clear. The dominant symbol of John Brown alone transcends
economics; his "Prayer" invokes the further aid of the God who
has already ordained the deaths of five men for "a man of iron
tears / With a bullet for a heart." Benét's account of the raid
on the Federal arsenal at Harper's Ferry, Virginia, reveals the
iciness of the zealot who could curtly tell his agonizingly
wounded son to die like a man. Brown, rapt in his patriarchal
pastoral dreams and oblivious to his responsibilities as military
commander, is part of Benét's portrayal; another aspect appears
in Brown's noble but deceptive statement to the Court, which
Benét quotes almost in full. Benét calls the raid itself foolish,
and his dwelling on the fact that the first two men killed in
the attack were freed Negroes underscores the tragic irony of
the abortive action. Brown had as his only gift for life, Benét
observes, the shepherd's gift; he was otherwise a failure, a
murderer, a fanatic with "a certain minor-prophet air."

Benét's interpretation does not stop here, for he sees Brown
as the instrument of history, whether one calls the generating
force of history mores, God, Fate, Man-soul, or economic law.
At critical junctures such a force will smash against a social
entity that has stood so long that it had seemed immovable;
it will

> . . . employ a hard and actual stone
> To batter into bits an actual wall
> And change the scheme of things.
> (54)

Such a stone was Brown, in Benét's view. After Brown's execution,
his body moulders in the grave, generating under the American
soil the spirit that will yet destroy slavery. Brown alive accomplished nothing; dead, as legend and symbol, he will conquer.

Benét's complex but balanced analysis of Brown foreshadows
the fairness and relative fullness of his picture of the South.
The Confederacy's courage and gallantry are given full credit
through depictions of imagined characters as well as through

those of the South's recognized heroes. The former cluster about the familiar Southern institution of the plantation. "Wingate Hall" and its masters are presented as romantic, in the manner of "that Waverly-streak that was so strong in the South" (120), as Benét puts it, with a reference to Scott's famed novel of chivalry in feudal times. Young Wingate reads Byron at midnight and thinks with pleasure of the Black Horse troop he will join, with its gallant name to charm a lady's ear. A year later, as a veteran on leave, Wingate goes for a canter and looks on the ancestral mansion, emblem of the South, as a shining dream. The aristocratic Southern vision was glowingly beautiful but tragically unrealistic. The Wingates are also somewhat spurious aristocracy: Clay Wingate is haunted by the tarnish of bastardy in his family, which traces back to the Duke of Monmouth, reputedly the illegitimate son of Charles II.

Also prominent in Wingate's mind is love of the Southern land, which he characteristically romanticizes and exalts above that of the North. Georgia's pines, rivers, and drowsy air Wingate loves the more because they contrast so sharply with the frozen Northern landscape. The South is for him a woman, beautiful, savage, and sweet, and his passion for it is the passion of a hot-blooded man for such a woman.

Wingate's conception of his region as feminine indicates the psychological and social emphasis which Benét places on the role of women in the South, a role deriving from feudalism. Two of the three supports of the Wingate family are women (although one of them is a slave). Ladylike Mary Lou, Clay's mother, controls the whole plantation; she performs the multitudinous tasks of womankind, as her mother has taught her to do, from supervising the slaves' domestic lives to childbearing. She is also charming, genteel, and flirtatious. Sentimentality underlay the Southerner's half worshipful, half lordly attitude toward his women. Benét also assesses the manner as half true, half false, and eroded by the war.

The feminine element in Southern culture is for Benét not merely a matter of sexual and social relationships; he sees the mind of the South as largely feminine. His view is implied by his choice of heroic couplets for most of the Wingate episodes. This meter, he asserts in his foreword, suggests dancing and riding, and the courtesy and dash of the South. However, the meter also has a feminine delicacy beside the more masculine accents of the blank verse and long loose line employed for the Northern episodes and the narration of the main action. In the President of the Confederacy Benét sees a girlish pettiness, a womanish inability to forgive; women will always have keener insight into him than men. Benét notes the predominance of the feminine in Richmond, capital of the Confederacy; it is a clannish city, thinking of the war as a family affair, devoted and jealous as the proud and lovely women who rule it. The South is its husband, Benét writes, extending the metaphor, but not wholly its master. Ultimately Richmond represents the entire South; when the capital falls, the Confederacy is finished.

When Benét focuses on Lee and his commanders, or on the feuding, clannish, fundamentalist hill people of the South, his cyclorama acquires broader scope and is made vivid through realistic detail and true perspective. A memorable description of the Army of Northern Virginia stresses the paradoxes and contrasts in its composition, which is summed up as "Aristo-democracy armed with a forlorn hope" (183). These "savage pastorals," Lee's army—fierce individualists close to the earth, rebels against the coming industrialism, a strange mixture of mountaineers, planters' sons, and poor whites, jesting, sentimental, but above all brave—became a legend exalted far above the truth. Its ranks also included deserters, cowards, and sadists. Yet there was truth to the legend; while many of the men came to repeat the bitter charge that it was "the rich man's war and the poor man's fight," they fought on with deadly courage. After all, they had Lee and Jackson: they were bound to win in the end.

Benét's picture of the Southern Negro is on the whole favorable to the South; there is no Uncle Tom or Eliza, nor even a mistreated slave, aside from some indirectly referred to as sufferers from a year-round hominy-grits diet (75). Two of the three Negroes to whom Benét devotes portions of his narrative have unique and valued status in the hierarchy of "Wingate Hall." Aunt Bess, the fat, aged mammy who is one of the three pillars of the plantation, has reared two generations of Wingate children; she is a matriarch, a tradition, "Half a nuisance and half a mother" (154). Benét sees her as a paradox, a maternal despot ruling through the force of tradition and yet still a slave. Enshrined by the tradition, the Aunt Besses yet shared with those who owned them a true kindness independent of their legal relationship, a "graciousness founded on hopeless wrong."

Cudjo, the other pillar among the Wingate slaves, occupies a similarly ambiguous position. Loyal beyond the coming of Sherman's army, uninterested in freedom, shrewdly judging white and black, privy to some of the white folks' deepest secrets, superstitious like all the slaves, scolding and scolded by his masters, Cudjo, the skilled major-domo of "Wingate Hall," helps bury the family silver when the Yankee looters approach (339-40). With it he buries his whole life.

Contrasted with Aunt Bess and Cudjo is another Wingate slave, Spade, a field hand. Well-fed, housed in a comfortable cabin, provided with a loving woman whom he loves, fond of all the Wingates, Spade nevertheless wants to be free and to see his children grow up free. He succeeds in escaping, full of dreams of bourgeois respectability in the North; but he encounters only hostility when he crosses his Jordan. He finally finds a family which succors him but he is forced first into virtual Northern slavery and then into the Northern army; while in this army, he receives a shattering wound. We last see him, subdued and humble, as a farmhand hired by Diefer, the Pennsylvania farmer. Spade's fate is an ironic commentary on the North's professed ideals.

Benét's picture of the North is less full and convincing than that of the South; indeed, his failure to provide an equivalent portrayal of Yankee culture and society amounts to a serious limitation in the scope of the epic. His principal character who represents the North, Jack Ellyat, is quite properly a New Englander, a boy from Connecticut; however, an evening glimpse of the Ellyat's living room, with the mother knitting, the father reading his newspaper, and a younger sister conjugating Latin verbs, is the extent of Benét's depiction of the family life of the region. Following a discussion of Brown's raid, Mrs. Ellyat prays for his soul and implores God to break the Southern people. A narrative shift turns her prayer into one of the innumerable prayers that Northern women raise so thick as to block the flight of wild geese through the night—"terrible, ascendent women's prayers" (50). That is to say, the women of the North, with their intransigent piety, were instrumental to the coming of the war, just as were the Southern women, with their delicate spurs of beauty and coquetry. But only in this respect does Benét develop a contrast between the social structures of the two societies.

Jack Ellyat is, of course, the Northern foil for Clay Wingate. We first see him out hunting (though in no mood to shoot) on the same day that Wingate goes riding on his plantation (19-24). As Ellyat savors the lazy enchantments of Indian summer, thinking a boy's idle thoughts, the poet interrupts his reverie with an admonitory ballad warning of the coming of war, the folly of complacency about the solidity of the Union, and the danger of resting his faith on the achievements of the Revolution while a tortured black ghost haunts the land. Somewhat troubled, Ellyat thinks about the South in a stereo-typed fashion resembling the way in which the Southern characters in the poem think about the North. Ellyat envisions the South as a land of Topsies and Uncle Toms, where the masters love their Negro mammies even though they sometimes sell them; where the girls are always beautiful; and where the men race horses, drink mint juleps, fight duels, and tar and feather Yankees. Ellyat comforts himself with the reflection that the crisis won't come to real fighting, that while he and his family may be Abolitionists, this allegiance need not mean the dissolution of the Union. In his rather limited way, Ellyat represents moderate Northern opinion of the sort that was Lincoln's chief political strength.

Benét directly states his estimate of the Abolitionists in a passage tracing the development of the war during its first year and a half (225-28). He gives them dubious credit for having engendered the idea that slavery must be abolished, even at the cost of war; but he points to the irony of their doubts about the idea once the Union is committed to it. He accurately appraises Charles Sumner, Senator from Massachussets and Congressional spokesman for the Abolitionists, as brave and strong but narrow and venomous. Benét depicts Wendell Phillips, the noted orator, as an intellectual bigot who would have divided the Union as readily as William Yancey, the Southern firebrand. But Benét, in restrained accents, also asks pity for the Abolitionists, "the pure in heart," who carried on the antislavery struggle for lonely years.

Benét's portrait of Lincoln contains no strokes unfamiliar to a reader of Sandburg's biography. Nearly seven hundred lines of *John Brown's Body* record Lincoln's wisdom, shrewdness, wit, kindness, doggedness, and courage; his homely speech and thought and his genius; his terrible loneliness in the White House; and his brooding on God's purposes in the war. Benét manages also to demonstrate Lincoln's growth as President, as the North moves from initial defeat to the conquest of Richmond, where Lincoln, with his rare sympathy, knocks at the door of George Pickett's home and identifies himself to Pickett's wife as an old friend of her husband. A short final section narrates with effective understatement Lincoln's assassination by Booth, the crazed murderer. Benét's portrait of the President is full except for being somewhat deficient in presenting Lincoln's ultimate greatness as preserver of the Union.

Benét's closest approach to showing the overall social composition of the North is his description of the Army of the Potomac (176-82). Like Lee's army, it was a human hodge-podge; its men were drawn from every level and condition of life and came from a dozen states which were not only different but alien to one another. Benét likens the Army of the Potomac to a huge sword forged from different metals and misused until it had to be reforged in agony. Unlike the Army of Northern Virginia, the Army of the Potomac suffered long from bad leadership; a good stallion, it was ridden against a hurdle of thorns by one uncertain rider after another until Grant took command. It never idolized Grant as it had McClellan; but it learned to trust him because he fed them and won, and because he had personal courage. The legends of Grant and the Army of the Potomac are inextricably intertwined, Benét observes.

Related to the North through the plot of *John Brown's Body* but philosophically distinct from it is the story of John Vilas and his family, who represent one element of the West and the Border States. They are linked with the main narrative when Jack Ellyat is captured at Shiloh and then escapes to be rescued by the Vilases in the Tennessee wilderness. The Vilases hide from the war, for they are morally unable to commit themselves to either side. John, the father, however, is more than an evader of issues; he is a philosophical seeker, forever on a quest for an elusive essence of life which he hopes to find in nature. Vilas has made his wife and family hostages in this search which began with a deliberate rejection of the values of the civilized East—specifically, the same Connecticut from which Ellyat has come.

Vilas personifies a philosophical element in American civilization which has its roots in eighteenth-century French thought, notably that of Jean Jacques Rousseau. The foremost exponent of this philosophy in America was the Thoreau of *Walden,* and Vilas is aware of his affinity with him. Vilas is also associated with Johnny Appleseed, with Faustus, with the Wandering Jew, and with John Brown himself, as well as other legendary seekers and rebels (325, 330).

The Vilas family is drawn into the war in spite of itself when Melora, the young daughter, falls in love with Ellyat and has a son by him, and again when Vilas' own son is forcibly drafted into the Union army. We last see Vilas in a half-ironic mood; he is partially reconciled to returning to civilization, for he realizes that his long escape has cost his family dearly. He has uprooted his wife from the secure existence in the East to which she was attached, and his only son has died in the war. Vilas now asks only to be buried "where the soldiers of retreat" lie buried, behind the fences of civilization. He symbolizes the ultimate futility of romantic escapism.

The full meaning of *John Brown's Body* can be uncovered only through a scrutiny of the central imagery. The obvious place to begin, aside from the function of John Brown himself as a legendary and historical symbol, is with the recurrent Phaeton imagery, which is another of the chief unifying elements in the poem. The significance of this imagery was first revealed by Paul L. Wiley in an illuminating article.[5] Taking as his starting point the comment by Henry Seidel Canby, in his Introduction to the twenty-ninth edition of *John Brown's Body,* that the Northern characters are more believable than the Southern because Benét endowed them with psychologies rather than mere "manners and fate," Wiley proceeds to demonstrate that the story of Jack Ellyat is a careful study in character development. The Phaeton imagery, Wiley shows, is used to indicate the phases of growth through which Ellyat passes, from romantic youthfulness to manhood.

Wiley also notes that the Phaeton myth furnished a supply of metaphors which fill the poem and that, since the myth has numerous associations, especially with sun worship, it provided Benét with a set of auxiliary symbols. Wiley focuses upon the sexual implications of the Phaeton legend as seized upon by Benét, for example, by making the car of Phaeton a symbol of the male generative power which fertilizes rather than scorches the earth. Citing Jung's *Psychology of the Unconscious* and other works, Wiley interprets as obvious feminine symbols the images of the earth, the ocean, and the waters in the passage in which Benét introduces the Phaeton myth. Other images in *John Brown's Body*—horses, fire, sun, spear, arrow, and sword— are also sexual, Wiley observes.

Wiley did not, however, trace all the major ramifications of the Phaeton imagery—particularly the moral and philosophical meanings—nor did he perceive the extent to which this imagery unifies the poem. The multiple functions of the Phaeton myth require careful analysis, particularly since they bear upon the artistic value of the whole epic.

The imagery is embodied concretely in the small statue of Phaeton the Charioteer atop the clock in the Ellyat's living room. Jack glances at it just before the family discussion of John Brown's raid; he sees Phaeton driving his bronze, snarling horses down the gulfs of air until they smash upon the black marble sea under the weight of the brazen sun they bear. Jack is filled with envy; he would like to drive the chariot of the sun. But, he reflects, Phaeton and his steeds are immobilized, and so is he in his world.

> Not all the broomstick witches of New England [Jack muses]
> Could break that congealed motion and cast down
> The huge sun thundering on the black marble
> Of the mantelpiece, streaked with white veins of foam.
> If once such things could happen, all could happen,
> The snug, safe world crack up like broken candy
> And the young rivers, roaring, rush to the sea;
> White bulls that caught the morning on their horns
> And shook the secure earth until they found
> Some better recompense for life than life,
> The untamed ghost, the undiminished star.

(49)

Ellyat's comfortable world will not break up, he tells himself; he will sit in the family living room until the ticking of the clock has cooled his hot blood and he has become like his humdrum father. He is wrong, of course; four years of war will shake the land to pieces and see him wounded and imprisoned.

The full irony of young Ellyat's yearning to resemble Phaeton does not become clear until we return to the original Phaeton myth, nor does the significance of all the details in the Phaeton-clock emerge. I do not know that Benét drew upon Ovid's *Metamorphoses*[6] but the Latin poet is his most likely source. At any rate there are no discrepancies between the two versions. As Ovid told the tale, Phaeton was the son of the mortal woman Clymene, who told him that Apollo was his father. Eager to prove his semi-divine origin, Phaeton climbed to the sun-god's gorgeous palace and implored Apollo to establish his filial identity. Apollo readily did so and offered as proof any gift that lay within his power. Phaeton asked to drive the Sun's chariot and his wild, winged horses for one day. Apollo, repenting his rash generosity, pleaded with his son to ask for anything else instead, for Phaeton's destiny was mortal. The course of the Sun and his chariot was perilous, fearful even to Apollo, and his fiery horses were difficult to control. The responsibility of driving the chariot, Apollo warned, was a curse, not the honor and hope which Phaeton thought it. But Phaeton, burning to drive the chariot, rejected his father's sermon; and Apollo, placing his blazing crown on his son's head, gave him careful instructions.

The horses flew swifter than the wind; Phaeton, unfamiliar with the journey and ignorant of how to control them, dropped the reins. The riderless horses ran wild through the universe, racing to the top of heaven and then plunging almost to earth, setting it aflame. Fields were consumed, mountains and forests were set ablaze, great cities were destroyed, nations fell; even the god of the sea could not face the flaming air. At last the Earth-Mother raised her blackened face and prayed to Jove for surcease and for justice, lest all the Universe return to Chaos. Jove, calling on the gods to witness his need to save the earth, hurled a thunderbolt at Phaeton which blasted him from the sky and slew him. His body fell to earth and was buried by Naiads. Upon his tomb were carved these words:

> Here Phaeton lies who drove his father's car;
> Though he failed greatly, yet he ventured more.[7]

The philosophical theme of the Phaeton story is common in Greek literature in the epic and drama as well as in legend, and it recurs in Christian literature. It is the theme of mortal pride encroaching on divine prerogatives and being humbled by divine retribution. *Hybris* is the Greek term for the excessive pride of Oedipus and of Phaeton; the Tower of Babel story is one of the familiar examples in the literature of the religion which holds that pride is the deadliest of the sins. Phaeton, described by Ovid as "hasty, hot, proud," was spurred to seek proof of his godlike nature because his friend Epaphus scoffed at his claim. Although assured of his paternity, Phaeton insisted on the one proof that his father warned him not to demand: mortal man must not hope to do what only a god can do. Because Phaeton's arrogance disrupted the order of the cosmos, the king of the gods smote him.

Benét manipulates the Phaeton myth in complex fashion throughout *John Brown's Body*. His use of it is flexible and resourceful; he neither binds himself with it nor does he completely distort it. It should be noted that the imagery appears much more frequently in indirect form than in direct connection with the Phaeton-clock; also, much of it appears to be derived from the original myth rather than from the statue of Phaeton which Jack Ellyat contemplates in Book I. Moreover, although this imagery largely develops the philosophical meaning of the poem, it does not furnish a complete and consistent explanation of it. For one thing, some apparent parallels between the legend and Benét's epic are merely coincidental; at times a horse is a horse.

The significant aspects of the Phaeton-clock as we first see it are six: Phaeton himself, symbolizing youthful pride; his ferocious horses, representing untamed force set free, doubtless with the sexual implications noted by Wiley; the "trophy-sun," suggesting victory in war and also personal victory; the smashing of the horses upon the black marble sea at the statue's base, foreshadowing the catastrophe brought on by the arrogant pride of North and South; and the clock itself, whose symbolic value is obvious. (Benét associates Ellyat with it subtly, however: Jack's perception of the "frozen" attitude of Phaeton and his horses reveals that he equates time with action rather than with thought.) Finally, the clock and statue provide cosmic symbols: time, the sun, the air, sea, and rivers.

The Phaeton imagery has already functioned directly and indirectly in the Prelude. The slave ship is, of course, at sea, and the disastrous black sea of the Phaeton clock is augured by the vision of blackness which revolts the mate when he goes down into the hold where the slaves are kept. References to the blackness of Hell and to the Judgment Day which haunt the mate's mind provide Christian versions of Phaeton's punishment by Jove. The mate's sight of the king of the slaves, Tarbarrel, an "image of black stone," and his vision of a black-leaved tree growing until it blots out the seamen's stars sustain this ominous note. The captain's citing of the Bible as the divine authority for enslaving "the sons of Ham" provides another Christian variation upon the Greek myth's elements of divine edict and the scorching of earth; in this instance the pagan story comments ironically on the fundamentalist interpretation of the captain, who relies upon the familiar Southern rationalization.

The first direct use of the Phaeton imagery occurs when the mate hears "horses of anger / Trampling behind the sky in ominous cadence." These are the same horses that come like a torrent of wind to destroy the peace of Jack Ellyat's autumn day:

> . . . winged stallions, distant and terrible,
> Trampling beyond the sky.
>   The hissing charge
> Of lightless armies of angelic horse
> Galloping down the stars.
>
>   (20)

Benét expands the charioteer's horses into hosts of charging steeds in order to make the myth suggest war. The celestial cavalry is, however, described as "lightless" in order to recall the waywardness of the sun during Phaeton's hapless ride. The term also suggests the lack of wisdom that he evinced and that the North and South displayed in letting passions whip them into the field. The adjective "angelic" stresses the horses' divine function and leads to the admonitory ballad already referred to.

This ballad, with its warnings against national complacency, contains explicit references to the Phaeton myth. These occur in the parenthetical lines of the ballad which are spoken by "ancestral voices prophesying war." Jack is addressed as "son," recalling Apollo's warnings to Phaeton; though the trees in the garden are strong, they shake; thunder sounds; lightning flashes; the sky falls. As the ballad ends, the thought strikes the startled Ellyat that the celestial horses are flying south; "the riderless horses never bridled or tamed" scream like eagles as they gallop "to trample the indolent sun." Who, he wonders, could have freed them to carry their portents across the Union?

With a surprising and delightful shift in his equine imagery, Benét (still presenting Ellyat's thoughts) likens the new states of the West, where the frontier rolls towards the sun, to wild mustangs to be ridden only by men with iron thighs and lean hearts. In this passage Benét keeps a tether on the Phaeton imagery through references to the mustangs, the sun, the moon, the stars, the skies, sunsets, riders, and gods; but all these images are juxtaposed with fresh and vivid Western images or, as with "mustangs" and "vaquero gods," are transmuted from their Greek form into an American mythology.

Ellyat's semimystical and prophetic moment is paralleled by that of Clay Wingate as he pauses in his canter about his plantation. He is stricken, even aged psychologically, as he hears the invisible cavalry riding the wind. Benét leaves Wingate to chant a song which links the portents heard by Ellyat and the Georgian with those sensed by the mate in the Prelude. The ominous horses in the sky, "burning-hooved," head for the sea; and the references to the other chief domains of the world—the air and the earth—sustain the cosmic significance of the original Phaeton myth and relate it to the imminent mortal war. The passage serves also to provide a transition to John Brown, the dominant symbolic figure of the poem.

At fairly regular intervals throughout the epic, Benét directly links Ellyat with the nexus of the Phaeton-clock. As Ellyat marches off to war down the main street of his home town, he reflects that his departure is too hurried and confused; it is not like Phaeton's heroic charge at the sea. Phaeton does not enter Ellyat's mind when he first sees action at Bull Run, but at the battle of Shiloh, just before his capture, he sees a huge horse, uttering a "frozen scream full of hoofs," rise menacingly above him and hang suspended for a moment (124). When the horse falls, it jars "the world." Marching in a column of prisoners, Ellyat reflects that this is indeed war; Phaeton and his bronze chariot are rolling across the sky. Escaping and lying half-asleep in the rain, he drowsily imagines that he is a Germanic hero lying in front of Nibelung Hall, having fallen there from the sky " 'In a wreck of horses, spilling the ball of the sun' " (128). Here Ellyat's drowsy mind confuses Greek and German mythology.

The lyrical "Song of Ellyat's Heart" (142-43), which comes as Ellyat and Melora Vilas consummate their love and conceive their child, reworks the Phaeton imagery to infuse it with sexual passion. Phaeton becomes a god of love, "Terrible beauty in armor"; time loses its power when the charioteer sweeps across the sky toward the moment of ecstasy. Ellyat is awed by the power of the god of love, who has awakened the sun. Phaeton has been dragged from the sky and "broken . . . with an ocean" because he has conquered, but he still sows passion (represented by his steeds) on the earth. Yet his conquest is momentary; the summit of love and passion exalts men far above ordinary life but they soon sink back into the familiar peace of the routine.

Ellyat's next apprehension of Phaeton, which serves primarily to keep the imagery in the reader's mind, comes after his release from a Confederate prison. In the family living room, Ellyat notes that although all else has changed, the charioteer on the clock remains the same. Ellyat reflects that this is the second time he has met the drunken charioteer and that there will probably be a third time before the war's end.

His expectation is borne out at Gettysburg. Here, however, Phaeton is transformed into a symbol of fate. This shift has been prepared for by Benét's assertion that the encounter between Lee and Meade was not willed by the generals but by a blind, deaf fate riding on a lunging horse (276-77). On the morning of the second day of battle Ellyat wonders what Phaeton has in store for him. It is a wound; lying half-delirious on Cemetery Hill, after fighting bravely, Ellyat looks up at the sky to see the chariot in full career:

> The yellow moon burst open like a ripe fruit
> And from it rolled on a dark, streaked shelf of sky
> A car and horses, bearing the brazen ball
> Of the unbearable sun, that halted above him
> In full rush forward, yet frozen, a motion congealed,
> Heavy with light.
> (298)

Near death, Ellyat interprets his vision as representing a toy death above the battlefield; his fevered mind imagines that he has risen into the sky where Phaeton can fatally wound him. But "something jagged" fits into Ellyat's heart, and he survives. The jagged thing is a piece of his essential self, of his manhood, which he had lost when he behaved ineptly at Shiloh and was captured. He had known that he had lost his integrity and that he must restore it. Thus in the two battlefield episodes involving

Ellyat, Phaeton emerges in a new guise, that of enigmatic master of personal destiny.

Phaeton undergoes his final metamorphosis in meaning for Ellyat when he is reunited with Melora at the end of the war. His wounds still healing, Ellyat walks from town in a meditative mood on an early spring day when the ice is melting in the sun, and he recalls the clock in the house "ticking its fettered time / To fettered Phaeton" (359). He attempts to reconcile himself to the loss of love and to a conventional life, musing that "Only a fool drives horses in the sky." When he suddenly sees Melora emerging from the wood with the sun behind her, the fetters fall from the clock of Phaeton, which is also Ellyat's clock. The humdrum life he has been contemplating, the war, and his wounds were the mere semblance of Phaeton; love restored is the reality of the charioteer.

Phaeton thus finally emerges as the symbol of Ellyat's self-realization and of the fulfillment of both his nature and his destiny. Ellyat's recognition of Phaeton's true significance disproves his conclusion that only a fool drives horses in the sky; he himself has dared and finally won. But even as Ellyat waits for Melora and thinks of returning to the West with her, the spring wind burns his flesh, a reminder of the perils of youthful rebellion against divine law and of the limitations of mortal man.

John Brown is similarly associated with the myth after his hanging, for Benét ironically observes that the Kansan will not again come "with foolish pikes / And a pack of desperate boys to shadow the sun"—that is, to follow in the path of rebellion (58). As prologue to Brown's unrepentant final speech to the court, Benét describes him as lacking any gift for life but knowing how to die; the law gave him six weeks to burn this knowledge in "one swift fire whose sparks fell like live coals/ On every state in the Union" (54). The speech itself Benét likens to "the insolence of the sun cast off."

The Phaeton-clock is also recalled in lines dealing with Judith Henry, the aged bedridden woman killed during the first battle of Bull Run: "She has known Time like the cock of red dawn and Time like a tired clock slowing" (87). Just before her death she hears not the tick of her kitchen clock but "in the sky a vast dim roar like piles of heavy lumber crashingly falling," a simile evoking Phaeton's precipitate plunge through the heavens.

As a final example of the hundred or more direct and indirect Phaeton images, there is the description of Lincoln walking in Richmond after its fall. In this passage images of the burning of the city, with red light falling on the President from the red sky, parallel the scorching of the earth and the destruction of great cities in Ovid's tale, while mention of a gang of looters opening a whiskey barrel in a red-lit square connects the scene with Benét's drunken charioteer.

Another important source of imagery in *John Brown's Body* is stones. There are two main classes of stone metaphors: those apparently derived from Ovid's legend, in which Phaeton is killed by one of Jove's thunderbolts; and those related to the fugitive essence of the wilderness, especially that of the West. These stone images do not function with the consistency and logic of the primary Phaeton-clock images, but they are collectively meaningful and provide the epic structure with another unifying device.

As pointed out previously, stone imagery occurs in the Prelude, and John Brown is somewhat ambiguously associated with supreme divinity, or with the impersonal motivating energy of history, in the passage in which Benét likens him to the "hard and actual stone" employed by the supreme force during crises. The Phaeton myth is recalled at the beginning of this passage, with the references to "a crack in Time itself" and to the earth "torn by something blind." When the force operates, it uses as its instrument "a hard and actual stone" to effect its changes. Such a stone was Brown, the poet declares; he was unreasoning, destructive, perhaps heroic, but "eroded to a cutting edge," with a gift for dying yet none for living. The framework of justice in which this passage occurs suggests Jove's punishment of Phaeton. Benét enters the poem personally to describe the courthouse, symbol of law and justice, and the account of Brown's trial follows. At its conclusion, some sixty lines sing of his death and prophesy his rebirth as a conquering legend for the North. To the poet's question as to why war must inevitably come, Brown's soul answers:

> *"Ask the tide why it rises with the moon,*
> *My bones and I have risen like that tide*
> *And an immortal anguish plucks us up*
> *And will not hide us till our song is gone."*
>
> (60)

These lines clearly associate Brown's avenging spirit with cosmic elements and processes.

The stone imagery is sustained, though altered, in Book II, "The Stone in the Pool." Brown's soul begins to march after the fall of Fort Sumter: *"The stone falls in the pool, the ripples spread"* (63). Benét ingeniously connects the stone imagery with the chariot imagery by following the italicized line with a description of the joyful frolicking of a colt belonging to Sally Dupré. A creature of the month of April, delighting in life, the proud colt recalls Phaeton's steeds in his wildness and fleetness; there is the look of folly and youth in his eyes. His name is Star, another echo of Phaeton's celestial ride. As Sally, hot-eyed with news of the fall of Fort Sumter, summons the colt, Benét compares the two in their grace in repose. The pair is also to be associated with Jack Ellyat and Clay Wingate because of their common youth, pride, and folly. After the vignette of the meadow, Benét links the stone imagery and the Phaeton imagery in a short transitional passage:

> *The widened ripple breaks against a stone*
> *The heavy noon walks over Chancellorsville*
> *On brazen shoes, but where the squadron rode*
> *Into the ambush, the blue flies are coming*
> *To blow on the dead meat.*
>
> (64)

The personification of noon is still another indirect reference to the sun and the passage of time.

The richest application of the stone imagery appears in Book II after an extended description of a map of the country in which the population markings are likened to iron filings (77-78). The filings are pulled from their normal patterns by the power of a "thunderstone" that has fallen on the land. A thunderstone is a rounded stone or meteorite once thought to have been hurled to earth by thunder and lightning; it thus calls to mind Jove's thunderbolts, one of which felled Phaeton. Benét strengthens the mythological connection by referring to the thunderstone's "blinded force" which emanates from a dead star but enables it to control human life. Benét poses two alternatives:

> If it is
> An enemy of the sun who has so stolen
> Power from a burnt star to do this work,

> Let the bleak essence of the utter cold
> Beyond the last gleam of the most outpost light
> Freeze in his veins forever.
>
> But if it is
> A fault in the very metal of the heart,
> We and our children must acquit that fault
> With the old bloody wastage, or give up
> Playing the father to it.
>
> (78)

That is to say, if some supernatural evil force—as opposed to the divine order represented by the sun—is responsible for the war, let us curse this force; but if the cause of the war lies within the American heart, we must pay the old bloody costs of war or renounce the ways which have sanctioned it. The second alternative is clearly the one to be accepted, but the Phaeton imagery has again served a useful purpose.

There are several minor variations on the stone imagery (for instance, Pickett's Second Corps advancing at Gettysburg is likened to a sea torn by stones flung from the sky), but the remaining important usage is that of the Wilderness Stone. Regionally speaking, the Wilderness Stone stands for the American West; in respect to plot, the Wilderness Stone symbolizes the Vilas family, especially the father. The Stone furnishes the title for Book III, in part because Grant's Army of the Tennessee, in which Jack Ellyat has enlisted, is composed of Midwesterners, but primarily because the last half of the book deals with the Vilases.

The narrative and philosophical roles of Vilas and his family have already been discussed: these wanderers personify the strong though fading element in American life which has its strongest affinity with nature, as both the source of life and the best setting for the living of it, and its strongest antipathy for civilization and its laws. The Vilases are "hiders." John Vilas is first described as having "burnt dreams" in his eyes and as having been in his youth a runaway colt who broke the pasture bars in order to "test the figments of life on a wild stone" (135). Again images of burning, rebellion, and daring recall Phaeton.

It is, however, the impact of the Wilderness Stone that has shaped Vilas' character and moulded the contours of his face. It has made him hard while giving him something which is not hard and which he cannot define for himself. He compares himself with Faustus; both of them are old and the bright devils of their youth have vanished, but they still possess some of their young rebelliousness were there sufficient cause for action. Vilas senses the love developing between his daughter and Ellyat but resolves not to oppose it. He is aware of the presence of the Stone in Melora but hopes that she will merely use it temporarily as a touchstone to distinguish good and evil and that in time she will outgrow her father's limitations. Vilas feels that his finding of the Wilderness Stone has been mostly in vain; such men as he are "Moth-light and owl-light and first dayspring men, seekers and seldom-finders of the woods" (248).

The screams of Melora as she gives birth to Ellyat's son bring to Vilas the poignant realization of the inescapable burdens of life and of civilization. He remembers the screaming of his wife as she gave birth to Melora, and a terrible old woman who sat beside him and cursed him with her eyes at each inevitable scream; and he thinks of the agonizing chain of cries reaching endlessly back into the history of mankind. His wife, he finally admits to himself, has always had a harder lot than his; in a moment of insight he perceives that, while he and his daughter see only pain itself, his wife distinguishes between different kinds of pain. Some types of anguish are blessed because they are within the law; some are cursed because they are outside of it.

Vilas' compassion for his daughter's present suffering leads him to pray for the second time in his life, although he prays for mercy for Melora only to seekers of the Wilderness Stone and to Nature herself. His prayer is answered after her child is born when rain eases her into sleep "hand-fasted to the Wilderness Stone" (250). In the end Melora returns with her son to civilization and to the child's father. Their love has flowered outside of marriage and the law; presumably (Benét does not specify) it is to be sanctioned, although Ellyat is bent on their returning to the West. Vilas, chastened by the death of his son (who could not escape civilization's war) protects Melora on her journey. His grieving wife, unwilling to remain with him, has already returned to her home in the East.

Vilas now knows that men who seek the Wilderness Stone should not marry or beget children; if they do, they may commit a wrong more serious than any intention of giving pain. His abandonment of his long, ambiguous, rather narcissistic idyll in the wilderness is an integral part of the meaning of *John Brown's Body* as an epic of American civilization upholding law and order. The Wilderness Stone imagery and the thunderstone imagery are related as manifestations of divinity: the first as symbol of divine power that man should not seek to possess, and the second as symbol of divine punishment that man brings upon himself by his arrogance.

A final significant image cluster in Benét's epic is constituted by seeds, which have a variety of meanings arising from this simple natural symbol of birth. The most prominent form of seed imagery is human reproduction. Melora, carrying Ellyat's child in the autumn, thinks of the succession of the seasons and dreams of the return of her lover in spring; she identifies herself with the fertility cycle of nature:

> "I am the seed and the husk. I have sown and reaped.
> My heart is a barn full of grain that my work has harvested.
> My body holds the ripe grain. I can wait my time."
>
> (223)

Melora's fruitfulness is a happy contrast with the initial seed image in the Prelude in which Captain Ball claims that he and the other slavers are doing the Lord's work, spreading his seed. The mate's augury of stolen black seeds falling on the fertile American land and, in the spring, growing into a huge tree blotting out the stars tells of the true issue of the slavers' labor.

Between the planting of slavery in America and the budding of Melora, seed imagery recurs in several forms. Wheat serves as a national symbol: John Brown's men look like (but are not) "good American wheat, firm-rooted, good in the ear" (32); Northern and Southern volunteers at the outbreak of war are likened to ripe wheat and corn (70). Wheat and iron represent the North on the strategic chessboard of war; cotton, "the fable throned on a cottonbale," stands for the South. Vilas' spiritual travail while his daughter is in labor unites the endless cycle of human birth with cosmic images; it continues, he thinks,

> Brighter than steel, because earth will be earth
> And the sun strike it, and the seed have force.
>
> (247)

The upheaval of the globe described in the Phaeton myth is again evoked by the poet's prophecy, after the execution of John Brown, of the anger of the ripe wheat and the quaking of the earth with the stamping of ghost feet (60).

These lines follow the identification of Brown's mouldering body with seeds which the poet hears growing secretly in the entrails of the earth. The imagined replies and prophecies of Brown's soul proliferate with images of spring: freshets and mountain brooks overflowing their banks, the rain and the wind stirring seeds into life. The gigantic myth of the corporeal death and spiritual rebirth of Brown, which Benét employs as his dominant myth, is thus largely conveyed through nature symbols. It becomes an American version of the ancient Egyptian myth of Osiris and the Greek myth of Dionysus.

In the final section of his epic, "The soul rests," Benét projects the myth of Brown into modern American and sums up its meaning. Benét pronounces a *requiescat in pace* for the feudal South; bury it, he urges, beside John Brown. Appraising Brown for the last time, the poet again calls him a stone hurled as a missile, "a sacrificial instrument of kill." But mindful to give Brown his due, Benét reminds us once more of Brown's love of the land, his "shepherd's gift."

Brown's feeling for the soil provides the symbol for his final rebirth in the poem: from his bones Benét sees growing modern industrial America, with its skyscrapers, great cities, and factories. Our productive power Benét likens to a genie whose might "we have raised to rule the earth." The phrase is ambiguous, but Benét makes it clear that the genie is already half our master. Transmuted into a portentous flame, it hovers over the land, "the engine-handed Age" of sorrows and splendors. It is, we perceive, the twentieth-century equivalent of John Brown, the symbol of division of an earlier age. Now at the last Benét epitomizes his historical lesson, the wisdom he derives from his story and offers to America.

It is the old but difficult wisdom of reason and moderation. Man should neither fear nor worship the genie of the flame; he should stand alone and contemplate it. (The passionate haters and the violent partisans of John Brown were equally wrong in their extremism.) The flame is potential evil and potential good; but the roots of both good and evil are within the observer's mind. Let the prophets of unreasoning despair and the prophets of unthinking complacency cry out as they will; but we must maintain our distance and keep our souls intact from them. If our hearts react so hotly to the central issue of our age that we cannot remain aloof, we should strive after the pain of involvement to make our hearts whole again by recapturing their purest essence. We should call the flame neither accursed magic nor a blessing, but merely accept its presence with quiet realism.

Benét's balance, moderation, courage, his consistent readiness to face up to complex truths all along the line and to accept the responsibilities of action, are qualities that parallel those in the liberal democratic tradition which embraces Lincoln, Whitman, and Sandburg. Benét's political philosophy is reflected throughout *John Brown's Body* by his unwavering concern for humane values and for the individual. This solicitude lies behind his condemnation of ante-bellum Southern ideals and social structure and his equally strong criticism of Northern antislavery zealotry. Thus Benét pauses in his account of the raid on Harper's Ferry to speculate about a Mr. Brua, who is mentioned briefly in one of the contemporary chronicles because, although he was one of Brown's prisoners, he picked up one of Brown's men who had been wounded, carried him to a doctor, and then, unbidden, quietly returned to take his place as prisoner. The action makes Benét think of Mr. Brua as "curiously American," and he muses about him for thirty lines, touched by this unobtrusive humanitarianism amid the violent follies of the raid.

Just previously Benét in a more somber mood has wondered what the souls of the two free Negroes who were the first to be killed in the raid might have said to each other on their way to heaven. The Congressmen armed with speeches and picnic baskets who came to watch the first battle of Bull Run as though it were a Roman circus draw from Benét only mocking irony. With gladiatorial salutes of "Ave, O Congressmen!" he hails the Iliad gods enveloped in their sacred clouds of "Floridawater, wisdom, and bay-rum" (88). Some eighty lines flay with unrelenting precision these representatives of popular government in their roles as complacent spectators at the bloody madness of Bull Run.

It is indeed the tragic waste, the terrible suffering, the insane confusion, the brutal irrationality of war that Benét emphasizes, not the heroics. He shows the great courage on both sides, but he shows too the way the fury of combat seizes some soldiers who distinguish themselves. The Black Horse Troop fights with hot hatred at Bull Run, and Clay Wingate savors their triumph; but, coming on the litter of the Yankee retreat and a cat slain in the fighting, he sickens and loses his taste for souvenirs. Jack Ellyat's experience of war, like that of Stephen Crane's hero in *The Red Badge of Courage*, is diversified; but always it contrasts harshly with his romanticizing of Phaeton-like daring. The field at Bull Run appears to him like a "deadly fair" with strange crowds rushing about and strange drunkards lying on the ground. At Shiloh he runs and is ignominiously captured; in prison he nearly goes mad and dies. Only at Gettysburg does he redeem himself. After some initial apprehension, he fights bravely but, like his Southern counterpart in the epic, hot-headedly. For Benét, "heroism" means passion and violent action.

IV *Romantic Love, Historical Realism*

Although Benét's depiction of war is unwaveringly realistic, his conception of love is largely romantic. It may be argued that in this respect his romanticism triumphs over his realism since the two pairs of lovers are happily reunited at the end despite the perils of the long war. Benét's treatment of the love of Ellyat and Melora is certainly characterized by overabundant though often lovely lyricism and by improbable though not impossible fulfillment; it is idealized beyond the more plausibly presented love of Wingate and Sally Dupré, though it also has more interest. Both the love stories may, however, be partially justified on historical grounds: since the Union survived, there is some logic in the survival of the main fictional characters who sustain Benét's narrative. Moreover, love of man and woman is not unrelated to the theme of fraternal love which is implicit in Benét's concept of reconciliation of North and South.

The lovers remain, however, youthful types rather than individuals; and they suffer by comparison with the vividness and complexity of the historical figures that appear in the epic. This gallery of portraits is executed with precision, firmness, balance, and understanding. Benét reveals extraordinary insight into men who are accessible only through contemporary accounts and historical studies which are often misleading, incomplete, or contradictory. Through his intuitive grasp they emerge as believable individuals who are integrated despite their paradoxes.

Benét often catches the extra dimension of personality, the rare facet, the element of contradiction that make a man fascinating. Of Stonewall Jackson, "wrapped in his beard and his silence, / Cromwell-eyed," Benét observes that he was the only one of Lee's generals who had a "strange, secretive grain of harsh poetry" hidden in him (187); it gleamed in his last words: "'Let us cross the river . . . and rest under the shade of the trees.'" Jackson's remark that Lee was the only man he would follow blindfolded, Benét seizes upon as a clue to a Lee who was much more than the marble image conceived of by some. Jackson's strength was hammered; Lee's was that of grace and proportion. Yet Lee kept his essence a secret hidden from all his biographers. Benét points to a single phrase for what depth of perception it affords: "'I'm always wanting something'" (191). This clue Benét interprets as revealing an inner force that ran counter to the prevailing harmony of Lee's personality.

The fullness and the credibility of Benét's portraits reflect their historical accuracy, a result of his discrimination and industry. He read everything concerning the Civil War that he could find; *John Brown's Body* is based upon a great deal of research. Two noted historians have paid tribute to its veracity. Samuel Eliot Morison, requesting permission to quote from the poem for his fine two-volume *The Growth of the American Republic,* told Benét that the historical element of his epic was accurate in all details.[8] Douglas Southall Freeman, who read the poem in the course of his research for his distinguished biography of Lee, greatly admired Benét's work, commenting, "'He could have fortified even his casual adverbs with footnotes.'"[9] Southern critic Allen Tate, though objecting to Benét's very favorable treatment of Lincoln, was impressed by the other portraits and called upon professional historians to straighten out a distorted perspective in American history by following Benét's interpretation of Jefferson Davis.[10] Ralph McGill, editor of the Atlanta *Constitution,* said as late as 1957 that he knew of no one else who had caught the essence of the Civil War as well as Benét.[11]

The best example of Benét's skill at interweaving history and fiction in poetic form is his account of the battle of Gettysburg in Book VII. In less than fifteen hundred lines he renders, with masterful compression and brilliant focus upon essentials, both the strategy and human significance of the great and all but decisive engagement. An introductory section, serving as a prelude, recalls the rich pastoral peace of the fields and farms in the Gettysburg region as Benét saw it on a boyhood visit. The countryside had then the same ripe beauty that it had in the early summer of 1863, and Benét's quiet memory makes more poignant his account of the tragedy to come. He next analyzes the strategic situations of the North and the South, noting the South's declining prestige in Europe. Grant is besieging Vicksburg; and Lee, deliberating on the course of events, determines to throw all of his strength into an attempt to break the Northern army and carry the war into the North. Benét skillfully shows the major considerations that occupy Lee's mind as he weighs his chance "like a stone in his hand."

Soon the Army of Northern Virginia is marching through the heart of the Cumberland while rumors of its whereabouts shake the North; Benét's tight narration conveys the suspense of the crisis and extracts the sense of fatefulness in the accidental encounter of Meade's army with Lee's at Gettysburg. At this point, Benét pauses in his historical narration to show the approach of the grey army as it looked to a little girl out picking flowers in a field; as always, Benét is concerned with the individual point of view, not merely with the impersonal historical. The frightened child telling her mother of the terrible swords of the grey riders enlists our sympathy and readies it for its major involvement in the battle.

The next brief section brings us to the firing of the first shot, but it does so by pointing up the irony of the Confederate Pettigrew's making contact with the Yankees while he is on a shoe-foraging mission. The succeeding section again focuses on individual experience through the eyes of stolid Jake Diefer, the Dutch farmer in Meade's army who is aroused to fighting pitch by the realization that "'those damn Johnnies is on my farm!'"

The first day's battle is classified as a minor one, Benét comments, but more men were killed than at Bull Run. Among those who die, it is said, is a farmer who is mentioned in the opening lines of Book VII; he died, the story has it, not from a wound but from what he had seen and heard of the fighting. Benét observes ironically that the farmer should have reflected that even minor battles are no place for a peaceable man. The fighting of this first day is grim, piecemeal, inconclusive; Benét summarizes it and points to the Union retreat from the town of Gettysburg to a destined high ground outside of it. On the Southern side there had been a dozen *ifs*—but what happened, happened.

Before relating the action of the second day, the poet inter-poses a short account of the familiar conducted tour of the battlefield and the modern tourist's inability to re-create the reality of the struggle, which he thinks of as having been fought by men of bronze and marble. It was all long ago, the wind sings—and the tourist buys a souvenir paperweight and drives home. But there once was a real battle at Gettysburg; and Benét, with the aid of such easily grasped symbols as a fish-hook and a Maltese cross, makes clear to the reader the basic topography of the battlefield and the disposition and strategy of the contending armies. Having done this, Benét advises the reader to forget the map and imagine the long lines of men in both armies, sleeping, eating, drinking, writing letters, suffer-ing in hospital wagons, standing guard under the slow stars: one hundred and sixty thousand men on two hostile ridges.

Benét's narrative point of view during the second day's fighting shifts back and forth from Jack Ellyat to the overall bat-tle action, so that the reader gains a full comprehension of it as well as its meaning to an ordinary soldier. Benét balances his individual and historical narratives by focusing on Pickett's charge and the wounding of Clay Wingate on the third day of battle. Benét's technique is actually multiple narration: we see the battle of Gettysburg and the whole war from the point of view of the individual, both committed and uncommitted; from the point of view of the people and their leaders, the generals and politicians; and, finally, from the poet-historian's own point of view. Benét, in the didactic manner of Whitman, does not hesitate to accentuate his effects or to interpret events and judge men; and his reactions add another and vital dimen-sion of thought and feeling to his story.

Wide scope and variety—more history, in other words—are the harvest of Benét's methods; what is lost, in comparison with the sustained loftiness of the *Iliad,* is intensity, singleness of effect. Benét sacrifices something for the sake of his created plot: the story of Gettysburg is halted by a shift to the Vilas family. It is occasioned by Ellyat's being wounded; to heighten our sympathy and suggest the unseen families of all the combatants, Benét shows us Melora dreaming of her husband and holding their son. The digression is strained, and it weakens what it otherwise a finely handled episode. Yet Benét's technique is in a sense inevitable: he is the poet of democracy who must concern himself with great and small. He cherishes humanity and the individual and can present both the heroic and the humble.

V Poetic Method and Style

Separation of the story from the poetic statement of it is a necessary but arbitrary act of criticism, and much of the foregoing praise would be invalidated were not Benét's stylistic achievement in *John Brown's Body* of a high order. He demonstrates expert control of the three basic meters he has chosen. The traditional blank verse which he employs for serious episodes such as the soliloquies of Lincoln moves with dignity and force. The rippling heroic couplets which carry most of the Wingate episodes, as Benét explains in his foreword, he chose because they suggest the gallantry, the dancing, and the riding of the ante-bellum South. This they do with remarkable sensitivity; Benét is most consistently successful in handling this meter. What Benét calls his "long rough line" accomodates a variety of topics from the trifling to the grave. It comes closer to the rhythm of ordinary speech than to traditional meters. "Shake out the long line of verse like a lanyard of woven steel / And let us praise . . ." (70), Benét writes as the introduction to a brief elegiac passage, and the rhythm moves long and slow like a wave sent down a rope.

Basil Davenport regards this meter, with its loose five- and six-beat line, as Benét's solution to the problem—which he shared with other modern poets—of finding a verse form suitable for contemporary speech.[12] The crux of the problem is to achieve a degree of similitude while attaining the distinction which poetry must have. Davenport is correct in asserting that Benét was one of the first poets to attempt this, but he is on more dubious ground in calling Benét's solution the best yet found. Benét was still struggling with the problem in *Western Star* at the time of his death, and in *John Brown's Body* his line occasionally sags. On the whole, however, his technical achievement in this respect is impressive.

In addition to traditional meters and the versatile long line,

Benét uses several passages of slightly rhythmic prose to sum up background developments. These passages are not wholly justified by their competence and by the swifter pace which they afford for covering material not directly related to the main narrative. They occur only in the first half of the poem; apparently Benét saw they served no particular purpose and discarded this prose vehicle. On the other hand, his use of songs becomes more frequent as the poem proceeds. These lyrics add genuine metrical distinction and provide another pleasing variation. The ballad in Book I reflects Jack Ellyat's thoughts on the eve of the war with changing refrain providing the poet's responses. The "Song of the Hiders" in Book III is a hushed and delicate lyric expressing the lovely fugitive quality of the Vilases' wilderness life. The "Song of Ellyat's Heart" comes at the moment of love's fulfillment. A brief lyric in Book V indicates the passage of time, while Sherman's march to the sea is celebrated in the rousing accents of a Negro spiritual. These and other lyrics complete the impressive battery of Benét's metrical resources.[13]

His diction and imagery are striking even when the latter is considered apart from its complex meanings and interrelationships. Line after line is alive with sensory detail and rich metaphor. Benét's style is hardly flawless, however; occasionally he lapses into an inappropriate and derivative romanticism, as when he likens leaders on the eve of the war to "ponderous princes" drawing on their gauntlets and to captains donning their coal-black armor (65). Another bad habit picked up from romanticism is the use of an archaic word for its pseudo-poetic flavor, such as "frore" (27). Now and then the lines are merely prose, sliced and stacked, as in a passage on the battle of Shiloh:

> In the books
> Both sides claim victory on one day or the other
> And both claims seem valid enough.
> It only remains
> To take the verdict of the various dead
> In this somewhat decisive meeting of the block.
> (120)

Nor does Benét escape clichés and awkwardness. When Benét likens war to a chessboard (171) and calls the rising action "The Crowded Third Act" (Book VI) and the South "a failing

star" (272), he is falling back on too-familiar phrases. Several
times Benét slips in the attempt to render the meditations of his
characters, as in a semicoherent passage in which Vilas thinks:

> what I have sought that I have sought
> And cannot disavouch for my own pang
> Or be another father to the girl
> Than he who let her run the woods alone
> Looking for stones that have no business there.
>
> (247)

Lincoln in one of his soliloquies is made to strike a painfully
rhetorical note when, after recalling his supposed love for Ann
Rutledge (for which there is no historical evidence), he mourns:
" 'It fills me with unutterable grief' " (208).

Despite such lapses, Benét's language is prevailingly fresh,
clear, and tuneful. He selects American materials for most of
his imagery, lovely as bittersweet. He describes the first settlers
in America as "homesick men" who "begot high-cheekboned
things / Whose wit was whittled with a different sound" (4);
and this expression of the historical fact through native metaphor
beautifully achieves Benét's purpose of rendering the essence
of his story. The American landscape is mostly portrayed
through the same sort of metaphor; a New England autumn is
described as

> Wrapped like a beggared sachem in a coat
> Of tattered tanager and partridge feathers
> Scattering jack-o-lanterns everywhere
> To give the field-mice pumpkin-colored moons.
>
> (19)

Often metaphors are drawn from the more general source of
romanticism but are equally arresting:

> The dawn ran down the valleys of the wind,
> Coral-footed dove, tracking the sky with coral. . . .
>
> (40)

Benét's ability to characterize with a single stroke is note-
worthy. Of Clay Wingate he remarks: "When he thought of life
he thought of a shout" (26). When the mountain man Breckinridge hears a twig snap in the woods, "He was all sudden rifle

and hard eyes" (81). A Yankee scout "died in Irish when he went out" (242). Just-captured prisoners are seen "with their sick, dazed wonder / And the mouths of children caught in a blunder" (103). On the other hand, Benét can sustain a metaphor to Homeric sweep and Tennysonian richness and melody, as when he describes tired soldiers

> Laden with sleep as with soft leaden burdens laden,
> Movelessly lying between the brown fawns of sleep
> Like infants nuzzled against the flanks of a doe,
> In quietness slumbering, in a warm quietness,
> While sleep looked at them with her fawn's agate eyes
> And would not wake them yet.
>
> (122)

This singing quality is one of the chief beauties of *John Brown's Body*. One or twice it overflows the narrative, but more often it sustains or enhances it. Rarely does his poetry merit the epithet "patchwork colors, fading from the first," with which Benét disparages this aspect of his work in the Invocation. Nor is it true that in place of storm-bold words he presents beggarly terms: his style when not delicately lyrical, intentionally feminine, is soldierly, direct and incisive as a saber. The spectrum of styles and the dexterity and complexity of imagery which Benét exhibits in *John Brown's Body* are not surpassed by any other modern American poet.

Benét's full realization of his poetic potential came with his choice of a great American theme; and the confluence of his talents and interests was not accidental: one called the other into life. To his task, which Allen Tate correctly gauged as "the most ambitious poem ever undertaken by an American on an American theme,"[14] Benét brought his mature judgment wrought of liberal ideals and realism, both rooted deep in the American experience. The impressive weight of scholarship behind the epic was the final factor in making the work far more than the popular success which some critics, including F. O. Matthiessen, have seen it to be.[15]

Merely as a popularly acclaimed epic, however, *John Brown's Body* was extraordinary; Benét's biographer found it necessary to go back to the early nineteenth century—to Bryant, Whittier, and Longfellow—to find a poem which had been read so widely and so attentively by Americans. It demonstrated a deeply felt if generally unrecognized need for a national literature. If Benét's infrequent superficiality, his occasional stylistic lapses and excesses, his costumed heroes and heroines and their familiar roles combine to make unjustifiable an all-inclusive verdict of greatness, his epic is still touched today by the "ray of quick, American light" that Benét hoped for as his gift from the American Muse. It gives his epic a central radiance that should continue to illuminate it for both the serious critic and the common reader.

CHAPTER 3

The Novels: From Yale to America

ALTHOUGH Benét had published three novels—*The Beginning of Wisdom, Young People's Pride,* and *Jean Huguenot*—by the time he was twenty-six years old, and a fourth—*Spanish Bayonet*—by the time he was twenty-nine, he wrote only one more during the rest of his life, and that during his thirty-sixth year. His early period of high productivity reflects a spontaneous interest in the form, but Benét did not have to force himself to become a novelist as he did to be a short-story writer. In his first three novels his energies reached naturally for problems of American youth of the 1920's; his fourth novel, though set in the Revolutionary period, has a young American as its hero; and his final novel traces the lives of its protagonists from their childhood at the turn of the nineteenth century until their maturity during the 1930's.

Only this final work, however, is mature in conception, form, and style; Benét's talents as a novelist did not develop at the same pace as his gift for poetry or his hard-won ability for short fiction. His intermittently interesting early novels show flashes of expertness; but their interest, chiefly biographical and historical, is limited to the student of Benét or of the 1920's. His fourth novel is a competent historical romance, and a bit more as well: it also reveals Benét's increasing control over his medium. Only his last novel has both significance and artistry. Like his best work in other genres, it deals with an important theme in American history and civilization.

I *The Beginning of Wisdom*

Benét's first novel, *The Beginning of Wisdom*[1] (1921), started when he was a senior at Yale and completed when he was twenty-two, is semiautobiographical in that as a boy the hero, Philip

Sellaby, is sent by his parents to a military school which he loathes; as a young man he arrives in New Haven with a group of poems which he submits to the Yale literary magazine. Like his creator, Philip shows considerable promise as a young writer, though his academic career is erratic. His attempt to enlist in the army for World War I is frustrated by ill health, just as Benét's efforts to enlist were repeatedly blocked by poor eyesight. Philosophically, the novel takes its hero to the verge of a maturity that undoubtedly resembles that of the author.

More importantly, *The Beginning of Wisdom* is shaped partly by Benét's youthful inexperience, partly by youthful daring, and partly by youthful rebellion against a prevailing literary trend. Basically picaresque in form, the novel ranges from California to the East to the Southwest to the Carolinas and back to California; but nothing of a sustained American theme of the sort that Benét would later attempt emerges from Philip Sellaby's adventures. Fate and Philip's own lively intelligence, sensitivity, and intense involvement with life govern the narrative more than do the special qualities of American culture. In its wide scope and inclusion of a variety of American types, however, the novel foreshadows the later Benét. At the moment, the young novelist is concerned mostly with the psyche of his hero as he wanders over the land in search of his own identity and of meaning in life.

It is impossible to ascertain whether other aspects of the novel's structure arise from Benét's apprenticeship or from deliberate construction. Probably the handful of lyric poems and ballads strewn through the novel, particularly in the first half, grew out of both sources. Inserted without introduction or comment, they sound a poetic variation on an incident or theme in the novel; but, since lyric poetry aims at evoking emotion while fiction seeks to reveal character through action, mixing the two forms creates literary discord. Also contributing to the formal disorganization of the novel are the lists of background characters, parts of letters, and the recording—as for a literary journal—of fragmentary thoughts of Philip. Several lengthy excursions of a purely fanciful sort do their part to give *The Beginning of Wisdom* the quality of a miscellany.

Benét was, however, in conscious revolt against the dominant tradition of the realistic novel; much of the looseness of form of his first novel stems from this cause. He believed as early as

1920 that realism had become a cult which was yearly producing longer and drearier novels.[1] Realism had performed valuable services—" 'It has punctured some showy bubbles and instructed us with a wholesome medicine' "—but it was now stifling individuality. " 'It is time,' " he wrote in 1920, " 'for a considered and furious reaction against the modern realistic novel.' " He called for a return to "color" and "the grand manner"; and he commended some of the older, established writers, including Joseph Conrad, Norman Douglas, G. K. Chesterton, and James Branch Cabell.

The occasional playfulness and fantasy of *The Beginning of Wisdom* undoubtedly derive from the Cabell who wrote *Jurgen* and *The Cream of the Jest*. In three sardonically humorous dream episodes, Benét's hero encounters the three Fates—Clotho, Lachesis, and Atropos—but manages to escape them temporarily. The second time he does so, he finds himself in a Heaven which resembles the tinsel paradise of his boyhood imaginings. After denouncing this heaven and its grandly impressive anthropomorphic deity as shams, Philip plummets through the cosmos to a cryptic encounter with a beautiful girl who finally reveals herself as his soul.

The allegory of these episodes is too involved and yet ultimately too insignificant in the total meaning of the novel for full analysis in this study. The fantasy is superimposed upon the picaresque realism of the novel—a realism from which Benét could not wholly free himself—and, aside from the recurrent theme of irony, it does not adequately illuminate the happenings on the American earth. In other words, the philosophical relationships between the two worlds are fuzzy. However, the fantasy has some relevance to the main narrative and it offers some insights into Benét's mind that give an early religious perspective to the place of the American Dream in his mature thought.

The religious motif begins with a biblical epigraph that reveals the source of the novel's title: "The fear of the Lord is the beginning of Wisdom." A second epigraph, drawn from *Harkett's Slang Dictionary* (a work of Benét's imagination), defines the meaning of the phrase "put the fear of the Lord into" as "to astonish, to cow, to terrify." Philip in his youthful bravado defies the Lord, or disbelieves in Him, or even embraces diabolism. The grim underside of this philosophical coin is a corrosive irony, one which apparently obsessed Benét himself at times if we may judge from the dedication of his next novel, in which he thanks his wife-to-be for her frequent help for his "mind made sick with irony." In *The Beginning of Wisdom*, Philip praises irony in ironic terms drawn from the Bible: "Irony suffereth long and is kind, is not puffed up. Blessed are the ironists for none of them want to inherit the earth. Irony believeth nothing, endureth all things" (161).

The death of his beautiful seventeen-year-old sweetheart, Milly, from pneumonia, which she probably acquired from him shortly after their marriage, has plunged Philip into this worship of irony. His despair is extreme because both he and his beloved are incurable romantics. His audacity shattered, he is haunted by the fear of death, and his sense of irony is salted by the disparity between the real and the ideal which he constantly encounters in his wanderings across America. The sight of a prostitutes' row outside a mining town; his shallow father's posturings; the bogus art and personalities of Hollywood; the injustices and short-sightedness of labor, management, and townspeople in an industrial strike; and the death of his best friend in the war—all sharpen Philip's painful awareness of what *is* and its distance from what *might be*.

That the young man's fate does not deepen into tragedy is in the first place due to his sense of humor. "There is a complete grief and humiliation of the spirit that has no resource at all but a certain whimsy of laughter" (251), Benét observes, as his hero, stunned over word of the death of his best friend, laughs almost hysterically before setting off for the inanities of a Hollywood party. The same sense of disproportion that reconciles itself in Philip's multifaceted sense of humor manifests itself socially, economically, and politically. Although his sympathies lie with striking miners of the Industrial Workers of the World, he perceives that neither side has perspective, and Benét's satire scores both worker and boss. Philip's humor survives even the major episode of the strike and the subsequent rail-roading of the strikers out of town in a gross violation of American rights, and he finally regains sufficient faith in America's purposes to undergo an operation to enable him to enlist in the army.

Philip's philosophy as set forth at the novel's end fortunately goes beyond good humor and common sense. He formulates it to himself as he sits in a church which he sees as the husk of institutionalized religion; it lacks the vital seeds of living faith as exemplified by "the liberal heat and humor of mind that has made Mr. Pickwick an immortal and the mood of sacrificial libation and rejoicing in every fruit and mystery of the earth that saw Bacchus as young and a god" (349). But remembrance of Sylvia, his second love, and "the vast unreasonableness of life" throw him into an anguished final struggle with irony. After a chilling vision, rather like that of Ishmael in *Moby Dick*, of an empty and meaningless universe, Philip finds a measured faith, a kind of vague humanitarian idealism with an element of aestheticism.

> "There is something," he said steadily, "something better than my own sod. Something living as lightning and merciful as rain. Something neither to be adored as an image nor hated as a foe, but a thing to be followed like a banner through the bones and wrecked armor of all the faiths in the world. Something comradely and despised by prophets, something lordly that wears all beauty like a careless coat, something greater than myself for which I am ready to die forever, if it be necessary, but something that will not let the least senseless cell of me wholly die. I accept it, God or love or art, I accept it. And I am ready to search for it and serve it and glorify it through life and the fear of life forever and ever until I come to the eyes of Irony and the stupor of the end."
>
> (351-52)

As he finishes his meditation he sees the figure of Sylvia, the fine, mature girl with whom he is in love. She is praying, and he kneels and prays beside her. She seems to him—and the cliché is irresistible—the answer to his prayers.

The meaning of Philip's yea-saying is so smudged with metaphor and irreconcilable alternatives that one wishes Benét had contented himself with the simple allegory of William Langland's great fourteenth-century poem *The Vision of Piers Plowman*, which Philip lovingly reads during this episode and from which Sylvia quotes. Philip's resolve to imitate Langland and "walk as wide as the world lasteth" to seek Piers, the People's Christ, is more believable and moving than his subsequent muddled affirmation. But Philip, unlike Langland, chooses to seek arrogance as well as love. At the novel's end, Philip and Sylvia are in a cavalier mood, secure in the knowledge of the forty-odd years of life they have to spend "like the devil among the indolent sons of God, going to and fro on this earth and walking up and down in it" (359).

This sort of bravado could be presented with a satiric tinge, as plausible youthful inconstancy of attitude, but Benét goes so far as to ascribe a "buried wisdom" to his hero and heroine, and this final fluctuation of attitude must be assigned to the author's youthful instability. Throughout the novel he maintains control of his material only for short periods, and his ambition is so large and indiscriminate that the work is overstuffed. Ironically, in light of Benét's critical position, the realistic episodes are superior to the romantic ones. Benét was never to free himself wholly of his romanticism, which in certain respects stood him in good stead, but in *The Beginning of Wisdom* the vaporous imaginings of his hero are smoke in the wind.

Benét's style, too, is clogged by its excessive use of romantic imagery, so that a girl cannot merely mock, but mocks "with a voice like falling silver leaves" (358). Episodes wrought from Benét's own experience, such as his traumatic stay in a military school and his career at Yale, are vividly done, though the latter chapters suffer from uncritical undergraduate enthusiasm. Also well done are the random accounts of Philip's struggles to create poetry, though the extent of Benét's own involvement with romantic Hellenism may be gauged by the fact that Philip's major poem retells the legend of Io. The social recording and commentary involved in the strike episode; in the Hollywood chapters, in which Philip improbably becomes a star; and in the army episode, which stops short of combat, are mostly superficial but are stylistically crisper and more effective. A reviewer at the time of the publication of *The Beginning of Wisdom* might well have had an equal measure of hope and fear for the young author's future.

II *Young People's Pride*

Young People's Pride[1] (1922), Benét's second novel, was written when Benét was twenty-four and intensely in love with the charming Rosemary Carr, whom he married shortly after its completion. He had been parted from her, and their wedding had been postponed—agonizingly, at least for him—until his writing brought him sufficient money for marriage.[2] The novel reflects the author's private preoccupations in its celebration of romantic love happily consummated after the surmounting of obstacles. The novel also reflects the advice of his literary agent to write about young people of Benét's generation in the post-World War I era so as to capitalize on his special knowledge of them. Serialization of the novel, finally accepted by the fashionable women's magazine *Harper's Bazaar*, further shaped the novel: Benét followed the agent's advice not to take the lovers to bed before marriage. *Harper's Bazaar* was, however, sufficiently broad-minded to permit hints of license in background characters, a hero who is not chaste, and a cool-headed mistress who is one of the chief characters. The novel is thus the product of a variety of stresses, restrictions, and interests; it is not surprising, therefore, that it is marked by confusion of form and theme.

Literary influences—or at least parallels—are also apparent in *Young People's Pride*. The arabesque style and civilized satire of James Branch Cabell are imitated to some degree, and there are resemblances to the fictional world of F. Scott Fitzgerald. The two heroes and some of the other male characters are loyal Yale men, intelligent but halfway between innocence and sophistication. They banter about, and sometimes discuss seriously, love, marriage, art, youth, money, and morality; and they desperately seek happiness. The heroes' searches take the direction of romantic love but they also aim at self-fulfillment in an art or profession. Self-discipline and conformity to adult routine are, they find, difficult after the excitements of being officers in France during the war, but they have not been wounded either psychologically or physically; unlike their compatriots of whom Hemingway wrote, they are lost only temporarily.

The novel opens with a New York party of promising young Yale and Harvard graduates drinking Prohibition gin, and the action takes place mostly in the big city and in the fashionable watering spot of Southampton, Massachusetts. One episode shifts the scene to St. Louis, where Oliver Crowe, one of Benét's pair of heroes, attempts to win away his beloved from her stodgy Midwestern parents. As in Fitzgerald's stories, the East appears as the glittering region of wealth and high culture; across the Atlantic, Paris gleams as the still headier home of love and art.

It is toward Paris that Oliver and Nancy are sailing at the novel's end, conventionally wed and romantically happy. They dream of a Left Bank apartment where Oliver will write a novel while Nancy works as a fashion illustrator for a smart New York magazine and cultivates her talents as an etcher. He has quit his job as an advertising copywriter, and his refusal to go on prostituting his talent is the concomitant of his amorous achievement. Their marriage represents a triumph over " 'all the fat old people who told us we were too poor and too young,' " notably Nancy's hypocritical mother, who has tried to maneuver her daughter away from the perils of marriage with an unproven writer of belles-lettres. Mother's subjugation of her cigarette-loving husband to the status of a contributing member of the Anti-Tobacco League is a second manifestation of her baleful Puritanism and rampant feminism. St. Louis and Paris are, symbolically as well as geographically, the two poles of the world of *Young People's Pride*.

Puritanism also figures in the troubled courtship of Benét's other young hero. Ted Billett, an earnest law student, wants to get married but foresees years of struggle before he can support a wife in the style he deems appropriate for the rich girl he wants to marry. In moments of discouragement, Ted gets impulses to return to Paris and "go to hell like a gentleman," but he fights them down because he has finished with dissipation and knows that marriage is the worth-while thing for him. But the economic —or, as it finally emerges—conventional obstacle to his marriage is less formidable than his obsession with his sexual transgressions during the war. This deeply hidden "bitter and Calvinistic penchant for self-crucifixion" (179), as Benét describes it, drives him to confess his Parisian sins to his beloved Eleanor as a part of his proposal. The girl, though acknowledging his lofty motive in confessing, is shocked and deeply wounded. Rejected and humiliated, Ted essays an affair with the devious and alluring mistress of his sweetheart's wealthy father and is rescued, after further humiliation, only by the intervention of Oliver, his closest friend. Oliver, who has recovered from his own hurt pride over a temporary rejection by Nancy, similarily redeems Eleanor from her tower of moral superiority by maneuvering her into an admission of her deep love for Ted.

The novel thus presents pride as the tyrant of young people; it forces them into stubbornly maintained positions which they relinquish only after a struggle and tactful assistance from without. Ultimately, however, their good sense leads them to a new vantage point from which they can enjoy wedded love and pursue their art or professions. Ted's essential Puritanism brings him to the verge of tragedy—his would-be mistress perceives that he would even go to the devil with religious conviction—but his approach actually results in merely a ludicrous impasse. Oliver, watching the gay young people at a Southampton dance, murmurs "'the beautiful and damned,'" but he utters the title of Fitzgerald's novel with amusement. Benét's young men and women, like their more famous fictional contemporaries, seek and savor the ecstatic moment, but they accept its passing with wry good humor. Nancy and Oliver in love know that "the only thing worth having in life is the hurt and the gladness of that fire" (34), but an instant later Nancy observes that "'New York pavements certainly are hard on loving feet.'"

The mingled realism and romanticism of Benét's two pairs of lovers are not, unfortunately, sufficient to give them fictional identities. Ted and Oliver are crisply described at the outset of the novel; but, aside from Ted's war with his conscience, the heroes remain merely Yale men, unscarred officers, and gentlemen. The outlines of the heroines are blurred by Benét's sentimental romanticism, and it is impossible for characters who kiss "like children being good to each other—cloud mingling with golden cloud" (83) to engage any of the reader's interests beyond the satirical. Benét's poetic urge sometimes gets the better of him and submerges meaning and narrative, as when he likens Nancy's favorite colors to "the colors of a hardy garden that has no need for the phoenix colors of the poppy, because it has passed the boy's necessity for talking at the top of its voice in scarlet and can hold in shaped fastidious petal, faint-flushed with a single trembling of one serene living dye, all the colors the wise mind knows and the soul released into its ecstasy has taken for its body invisible, its body of delight most spotless, as lightning takes the bright body of rapture and agony from the light clear pallor that softens a sky to night" (30).

The one figure in the novel who escapes clichés of style and characterization is Mrs. Severance, the accomplished mistress, whose cool machinations and deadly insights do not deprive her of womanliness and even a certain pathos as she sees herself nearing the end of her beauty. At the close of the novel Oliver departs from her, painfully aware of her maturity and his callowness. The reader wishes that he had read more of her and less of Oliver. But even Benét's conception of Mrs. Severance is marred, for while she knows something of psychoanalysis and believes in it, she is unable to interpret her own obviously Freudian dream.

The brief discussion of Freud's theories by Ted and Mrs. Severance has some vague thematic connection with Ted's sense of sexual guilt and with the central theme of romantic love, but the connection is not logically established. Benét's failure in this respect is, indeed, generally apparent throughout the novel. As his biographer has observed, the chief fault of *Young People's Pride* is that it contains too many themes and unresolved ideas.[3] Benét's sensitive awareness of the problems of the postwar generation of which he was a part (although physical disability kept him from the military service which he eagerly desired) had too many facets, and none of them was given proper perspective in this novel. Hence its mood wanders from effusive lyricism to realism to satire and comedy. Possibly the inexplicable shifts from past to present tense also reflect some basic confusion of purpose. Benét recognized the novel's lack of merit; he told his fiancée, "'It is rather fluffy sort of stuff and I have farced it immensely.'"[4] Later he commented, "'Trouble with Y.P.P. is, some of it's real but much of it's rubber stamp.'"[5] The novel is partially redeemed by its single three-dimensional character, by its intermittent stylistic precision and liveliness, by its occasionally effective satire, and by its sporadically subtle insights into the minds of young people of the early 1920's; but its author's judgment of it remains essentially correct.

III *Jean Huguenot*

Jean Huguenot (1923) was begun as Benét's second novel in 1921 and partly written in that year, but was completed and published in 1923 to become his third. He admitted that it was difficult for him to write. "'I should have kept it much longer,'" he said after its publication, and he told his wife that writing *Jean Huguenot* in Paris in 1921 was like "'driving myself at a bar about 6 ft. too high.'"[6] The themes and even much of the style of *Jean Huguenot* could not have been predicted on the basis of either *The Beginning of Wisdom* or *Young People's Pride,* and Benét's problems in writing it probably stemmed from his entering fictional country that was not only new but fundamentally alien to him. The state of Georgia that Benét knew well forms the setting for the first part of the novel, and Southern decadence in the early twentieth century is a theme; but analyzing convincingly and individualizing a beautiful girl were overly complex problems for Benét at this stage of his career. Once again in commenting about this character he showed his critical insight: " 'My heroine is queer,' " he told his wife. " 'I can't be firm with her—I know too little about her.' "[7] And the theme of decadence had to await William Faulkner.

Jean Huguenot is one of the numerous fictional sisterhood of ravishing Southern belles. Benét's heroine is distantly removed from the Civil War, but she suffers from the ruinous consequences of the South's defeat. The novel opens with a satirical sketch of Jean's Uncle Tom, Major Thomas Audrey, the gentlemanly minister of a small, fanatical church of the town of St. Savier and the last representative of the old South. He holds his dwindling congregation by summoning up the vision of a Second Advent of huge plantations, well-treated slaves, bell hoop-skirts, and a South "like the fine, inimitable, fantastic thing that had flamed to pieces in the sixties like burning straw." After him, tourist hotels, Fifth Avenue branch shops, tea rooms and a country club would come to desecrate St. Savier.

The Major perceives that his seven-year-old niece is the last of the Huguenot line, which is decaying like St. Savier. The offspring of a third union with a family which with the Huguenots had produced only "queer, maladroit sports," Jean seems genetically doomed to a misspent life. And the child as Benét presents her seems destined for tempest and possible tragedy; she is possessed of a violent temper, fierce energy, and a frighteningly precocious talent for subjecting her uncle to her will. She does not, of course, remember her eighteen-year-old mother, who died giving birth to her, nor her father, a colonel who had been so exhausted by the Civil War that he had roused himself to marry only fifteen years after it. His bride was impelled toward him by the power of the Huguenot name, still a great one in St. Savier, and by her own consuming youthful impatience for experience. His marriage spurs the Colonel to make grandiose plans for consolidating the family cotton mills and for building a new wing for the family home, but he soon lapses into inactivity. He dies soon after his wife, leaving his infant daughter to be reared by her faded, withdrawn Aunt Eve.

In the one-tenth of the novel devoted to Jean's childhood, there stands out with considerable emphasis her infantile Voodoo worship. She has deified a wax doll which she had left in the sun and which had been partially melted. She prays to her misshapen idol, which she endows with powers of life and death, for blessings for her friends and dire ends to her foes. She croons to her Voodoo, exalting him above God. But she still fears the traditional Diety until He fails to strike her with a thunderbolt during a storm which she imagines He has sent to punish her. She dances a naked exultant dance to celebrate her escape, but the next day smashes her Voodoo because he has failed to silence God's thunder and has let Uncle Tom die.

Despite the ironic edge which Benét gives to his account of this strategically placed episode, the reader is prepared to take it seriously, either as the introduction of a religious theme or as an index to something fundamental in the character of the heroine. Yet nothing in the remainder of the novel develops either of these possibilities, except in the structurally unrelated sense that the heroine escapes traditional religious strictures when she violates traditional morality. In fact, it soon becomes apparent, as Benét swiftly takes Jean through her adolescence and young womanhood, that he is presenting the successive stages of her life as isolated phases. Benét tells the reader that Jean resents the coming of her puberty, that she acquires a sense of personal power which is augmented by her beauty; but this adolescence could characterize any number of girls.

When Jean is seventeen, pity moves her to tell an adoring boy that she returns his love, but this quality of sympathy has not been previously shown in her, and it is not stressed hereafter. The boy, rather implausibly, kills himself after she has told him she wants merely to be friends, and Jean suffers not only the feelings of guilt normal under the circumstances—though impulsiveness has been her only sin—but a cruel ostracism which is initiated by the boy's mother and sustained by his and Jean's former friends. Jean eventually lives down her reputation as "murderer" but the experience shakes her profoundly. Finally she summons her determination and decides to leave St. Savier to see the world.

The immediate cause of her departure, made possible by the death of her aunt whom she has been nursing, is her failure to win a love which at first she has not wanted. Gabriel Keene—a name which is perhaps symbolic, since he is witty and intelligent and blows the metaphorical trumpet that awakens Jean's love—is the dashing night clerk at the hotel. Well-read, intellectually curious, and an aspiring poet, he sees Jean as Eve, beautiful and passionate. Their relationship begins in avowed friendship, in accordance with Gabriel's theory that the so-called war between the sexes is nonsense. Six months of companionship bring him to an excited avowal of his love for Jean. Her beauty has been waxing to the point that she almost hates it, "for it seemed to be something beyond her control or will or knowledge—a burning dominance that she could no more shake off than her skin and that was now busy breaking the most liberal acquaintanceship she had ever known to bits with as little concern as an avalanche has for the ground it erases" (92).

Gabriel, whose conversation is entertaining but unrealistic, implausibly renounces Jean as he declares his love for her. They are basically incompatible, he tells her, and he has things he must do—he does not specify them aside from going to work on the Panama Canal. Jean, though previously unaware of the depth of her feeling for him, is so stung by the triumph of his practicality over his emotions that she screams the ultimate Southern insult at him: "'You—nigger.'" During the next four days Gabriel alternately elaborates on the wisdom of their parting and implores Jean for a final rendezvous. She finally consents, again moved by pity for him which surpasses her hurt. After their meeting is blighted by the approach of a lynch mob obsessed with avenging the rape of a mill girl by burning her Negro attacker, they part forever.

The lynching interrupts a moment of the deepest communion between the lovers, but it is an incidental lynching unrelated to the basic themes of the novel. It has a superficial connection with the initial theme of Southern decadence, but Benét establishes no direct and logical relationship between the regional violence and the decline of the Huguenots. The episode is the final and most serious instance of the disunity that mars the first third of the novel.

The other two books of the novel are better unified. Each deals with a love of Jean's. The first is her wedded love for Shaw Ashley, the New England history professor she marries eight months after the death of her aunt. The second is her adulterous love with Hugues Parette, a French automobile racer.

In these final two parts of the novel, Jean's initial resemblance to Flaubert's Madame Bovary becomes more obvious. She is the beautiful and romantic young wife who finds herself married to an unfeeling man absorbed in his work; when she seeks solace in illicit passion, it is only to be betrayed and to sink lower and lower morally and socially. And as with Emma Bovary, the society—or societies—in which Jean Huguenot lives is in some sense responsible for her decline.

Shaw Ashley is a latter-day Puritan obsessed with sex and work. He regards the latter partly as an anodyne to quiet his passion, which he feels is wicked. He has flashes of insight into history which enable him to rise steadily in the academic world, but he cannot understand his wife. Nor, despite his strong sexual drive, can he awaken her passion. He has been attracted to her originally by her beauty, but after possessing it nominally in marriage, he finds himself jealous of it in some way which remains obscure to him. Under his demeanour of self-control and absolute sureness—qualities which draw Jean to him as the polar opposite to the mercurial Gabriel—Shaw is essentially immature. Yet it is his addiction to his work that finally disrupts his marriage. Writing feverishly to exhaust the last iota of meaning from a sudden significant insight into history, he refuses to go at once for the doctor when Jean tells him that their young daughter, Eve, is seriously ill. His delay causes not only the child's death but that of Jean's unborn child.

The loveless marriage endures another year while Shaw spends his sabbatical year doing research in England and Spain. Jean is left to dull her pain as best she can, and she endures until she meets the charming Hugues, who is somewhat younger than she. She first sees him as the winner of an automobile race in Spain; handsome, vital, charming, and masculine, he reminds her of Gabriel. When he tells her that she has never known real love—"The love that is hungry and thirsty and full of hell" (213) —she is all but ready to run away with him. When Shaw refuses her a divorce, Jean goes off to live with Hugues in Paris.

Jean's new lover is "emotional, concise and direct in his dealings with men and women where Shaw had been logical, diffuse and surreptitious" (232). Hugues, who comes of a strict Protestant family, is deeply if naïvely religious; but he rationalizes his taking a mistress by saying, "Il faut vivre, il faut aimer" (231). This attitude Jean sees as illogical but agreeable, for she has finally found happiness. She feels herself fused body and soul with Hugues and imagines that they inhabit a bit of the fourth dimension. Benét even provides a catalogue of the elements of their happiness: "Desire," "proud as Pegasus"; "Ecstasy of the body like a burning flower"; Kindness; Faith; and Wit (229).

The happiness of Jean and Hugues lasts until World War I engulfs Europe. Jean assumes without much difficulty the clearly defined status of a Parisian mistress, fending off rivals who would like to supplant her lover. After a year Hugues honors her—she regards his offer as more meaningful than the marriage ceremony—by asking her to marry him. It means his lifelong devotion and the possibility of children. Shaw divorces Jean on the grounds of desertion, but Hugues has asked for her hand after the end of the war, if it has not crippled him.

Their happiness endures during the first few years of the conflict, until Hugues begins to crack under the strain of combat flying. He becomes increasingly morose or reckless during his leaves, drinks more and more, and spends less and less time with Jean. One morning about five months before the end of the war, she awakes with the certain knowledge that Hugues has been killed. With confirmation of her intuition—he has crashed while stunting in his plane—comes the further knowledge that Hugues has had a peasant mistress near his airfield. In his effects forwarded to Jean she finds a letter from the mistress telling Hugues that she is pregnant. It is a fair inference that the receipt of this letter just before Hugues's death was partly responsible for it. His recent instability can therefore be interpreted as arising from guilt over his deception and his divided loyalties.

The thwarted maternal love of Jean, which Benét has previously stressed in her love for her lost child, now takes the improbable course not only of her providing for Hugues's child by Jean's rival mistress but of debasing herself through prostitution in order to do so. She has set herself a minimum sum to earn, and she earns it in less than a year. The cost is utter loathing for herself, her occupation, and her associates. Her sense of integrity shatters. "'There was a young lady who loved in a blur,' she thinks distractedly; 'She had so many selves she didn't know what to do'" (262). She does not suffer from a sense of the immorality of her life but from its ugliness and meaninglessness. Only moments in which she sees in memory herself and the Huguenot house in St. Savier restore her to a kind of sanity.

Finally a letter notifying her that a maternal relative, spinster Miss Jessie Audrey, has left her five thousand dollars awakens once more her "deep, fantastic pride in her name and her race. . . . The Huguenots were over, but they stood by their own" (266). Yet her primary aim of providing for Hugues's son has been fulfilled, and she no longer cares for her life. Having degraded herself even further than Emma Bovary, though for an unselfish reason, Jean too attempts suicide. Unlike her nineteenth-century French counterpart, she is unsuccessful.

Before she emerges from the coma of her suicide attempt, she dreams that the chief men in her life have assembled at a personal Judgment Day for her. Benét develops the episode sketchily, though it would seem to be of crucial importance. Moreover, it is unclear whether the judgments arise from Jean's own dreaming mind or are to be taken as the author's verdict on his heroine. In any event, they are not merely the self-justifications of the men. Uncle Tom Audrey absolves Jean because she was so charming and disqualifies himself as judge because he was a lifelong friend of the Huguenots. Ricky Cotter, the boy who had killed himself for love of her, inexplicably declares that he had gone on living. He not only fails to blame Jean but asserts that he can imagine no Heaven without her. Shaw unexpectedly apologizes briefly and withdraws. Gabriel pays her a typically effusive tribute and also stands aside. Finally Hugues bitterly accuses himself. " 'She loved me and I hurt her forever. . . . She is the only one who is hurt of all us stupid animals—she who was not an animal' " (272).

The sound of a child's running feet which terminates this dream forecasts Jean's final courageous action in the novel. Before she takes it, she meditates in the woods near Paris and assesses her past and her present. It is her beauty and its effect on her that preoccupy her. She finds herself still handsome, but the "secret of the loadstone" has vanished. Yet she does not regret the passing of the peak of her beauty. Benét compares her to a king who has long wielded great authority and finally relinquishes it with relief. Her beauty had brought her "moments of ecstasy as immense and passing as the nuptials of an eagle. And it had very nearly broken her beyond redemption" (277).

Yet she could not feel sorry for all that had transpired. Had she had her life to live over again, she feels, she would have made fewer mistakes, but doubtless things would have gone much the same way for her.

This moment, which represents the triumph of common sense over romanticism, is followed by Jean's decision to adopt the son of Hugues. She finds him like his father in person and temperament, and responsive to the steadfast affection she gives him. At the novel's end she tosses a coin to determine whether they will go to France or America for the financially restricted but emotionally rich life they will share.

The difference between *Jean Huguenot* and most of Benét's writings, including his first two novels, is pointed up by the fact that, when Jean considers the alternatives for her and her adopted son, they are quite practical ones: "For France, the rate of exchange and a fair chance of paying work to do, since she knows the language so well. For America—a larger chance of better-paid work perhaps—less danger of a recurrence of the past" (288). Yet this prosaic realism does not attract Benét any more than it does all but the stolid reader. However admirable it may be as philosophical resignation, it cannot charm like Benét's metaphor for the qualities that compose romantic love: "Heraldic images that lovers make in their idleness, hanging them around the dark throat of Chaos like a string of carved beads, to mock his air of asphyxiation with bright colors and noble attitudes for a moment serene and brief" (229). We suspect that Benét, like the Flaubert who said, *"Je suis Madame Bovary,"* was in love with his heroine and sympathized with her romanticism more than with her mature resignation. Unlike Flaubert, however, Benét was unable to submerge his romanticism and fuse his style and themes in a common conception. Although *Jean Huguenot* is somewhat better unified than *Young People's Pride* and *The Beginning of Wisdom* and is altogether a trimmer, more carefully controlled work, it still lacks an articulated structure. As has already been pointed out, this failure occurs primarily in the apparent rupture between the initial theme of Southern decay and the subsequent emphasis of *Jean's* struggle with her beauty.

As a summary of the plot makes clear, Benét crowds this novel, like his others, with incidents, and the story is intermittently interesting. But the adventures-of-a-beautiful-girl sort of novel is hard to take seriously, and *Jean Huguenot* therefore becomes heavily dependent on character. As already indicated, the heroine is unconvincing, and so are most of the other characters. Next to his heroine, Benét analyzes her husband most thoroughly, yet he too remains rather hazy in outline. In our last glimpse of him we are told that he has a "heavy rear" (217), and the detail is startlingly incongruous. Hugues Parette seems somehow familiar, a too-typically romantic Frenchman. Some of the minor characters, such as Uncle Tom Audrey and Hugues's shrewd, greedy French mistress, are more vividly drawn.

The essential meaning of the novel, aside from the obvious significance of the Southern episodes, is that the old morality and the old religion are dead for Benét. The emerging new morality aims at fulfillment in love, both physical and spiritual; and it rejects—at least as an absolute—the formal demands of society for sanction by marriage. Sin disappears as a concept. Jean comes to believe that Hell is not the dark magnificence of Milton's Pandemonium nor the Burning Lake envisioned by the medieval mind; it is the garish, vulgar brothel where she makes herself available. She cannot regard herself as a really bad woman; she is merely officially so. Most men and women, she decides, are "not so bad"—merely childishly eager for delight. Even at their worst they would sometimes be kind. Jean Huguenot's burdens are those imposed by her beauty and her sex and by the thwarting of her feminine desires.

With none of these issues of the old and new morality and religion does Benét deal fully and forthrightly. Except for his refusal to condemn his heroine for prostitution, these problems appear tangentially as thinly presented conflicts of the postwar era but with their genesis far back in the nineteenth century. Benét's attitude towards sex and marriage somewhat resembles Hemingway's in *A Farewell to Arms,* but Benét merely suggests delicately and ineffectively that his heroine has fullblown sexual desires. Only the trivial and confusing dream of a personal Day of Judgment remains to supplant the old religion and its ethics. What survives for the reader is Benét's ability to project momentary states of mind with some insight and force, his occasionally perceptive study of his heroine's relationships with her arid husband and passionate lover, and his sympathetic awareness of the real elements that constitute the happiness her beauty promises but always denies her.

IV *Spanish Bayonet*

Benét's fourth novel, *Spanish Bayonet* (1926), which appeared three years after *Jean Huguenot*, reveals a marked advance in his control of the form. Unified in theme and structure, limited in its objectives, consistent in the mode and quality of its style, *Spanish Bayonet* is technically a competent novel—easily Benét's best up to this time in these respects. Its superiority is gauged in part by his rejection of ten thousand dollars from a publisher in order to keep the plot essentially as he wanted it.[8] He needed the money for his wife and daughter and himself; the editors of *Pictorial Review* were ready to pay that sum for serial rights; and Benét made some compromises in order to make the novel salable. But he could not resurrect the heroine he had killed off and marry her to the hero, and *Spanish Bayonet* was published in book form only, with its hero bereft at the end.

The novel represents an intermediate stage in Benét's progress toward using America as his central theme. The American Revolution serves as a background whose influence extends into the main action, which has its setting in pre-Revolutionary Florida. The still more exotic Spanish island of Minorca, whence Benét's ancestors had come to America,[9] forms the setting for the prelude, which introduces the hero's comrade-to-be, Sebastian. Andrew Beard is the younger son of a prosperous New York Tory merchant who suspects his elder son of associating with the Friends of Liberty. The father sends Andrew to Florida as his agent to study the colony which Dr. Gentian, a Scotch physician, has established below St. Augustine; Andrew is to evaluate its structure, methods, and products, and particularly its loyalty to the Crown.

When Andrew arrives at St. Augustine, he finds the doctor to be a learned gentleman with an air of command and a genius for colonizing. New Sparta—named after his entrancing daughter—has as its labor force three ethnic groups: Italians, Greeks, and Minorcans. These last include among them the engaging but hot-blooded Sebastian and the maidservant Caterina. A cool and remote Mrs. Gentian and a Mr. Cave, a loutish and ominous overseer, complete the roster of major figures.

The essential plot is the familiar one of an innocent arriving on a smiling scene which little by little proves sinister. Andrew inevitably becomes involved with the lovely Sparta Gentian, proposes to her after six months, and, with the approval of her father, is accepted. Hints of a covert terror and oppression under the surface of the colony are climaxed by Andrew's discoveries that his fiancée is the mistress of Mr. Cave, that she has a regal lust for power, and that her corruption emulates that of her father. Dr. Gentian is revealed as the sadistic Machiavelli of the colony, bent on keeping the Minorcans virtual slave laborers. Andrew attempts to rescue the persecuted Caterina by shooting Dr. Gentian, but his pistol fails to fire and he is imprisoned with Sebastian. The two finally escape, take Caterina with them, and attempt to sail in a small boat to St. Augustine. Caterina dies from a bullet wound, but Andrew lives to return to New York to join the Revolutionary forces in the fighting which has already broken out.

The story is deftly narrated, and Benét achieves considerable suspense through skillful revelation of character and situation. Despite these virtues, *Spanish Bayonet* would hardly be worth scrutiny were it not that certain elements give it values that take it beyond the market for the faraway in time and place, the cookie-cutter characterization, and the synthetic perfumes of the costume romance. This novel in a sense is a compromise between romance and realism, with the latter finally triumphant. The hero, though he tends to think too much like Benét—for example, he compares the wicked Sparta in the moonlight to a silver axe in a scabbard of black glass—is a plausible combination of youthful courage, idealism, sympathy, and ineptitude. His transition from a loyal Tory son to a Liberty Boy is convincing, progressing through a series of self-revelations which are intuitive rather than logical.

This progress is one aspect of Andrew's maturing, which takes him from innocence through awareness of evil to a young adult's sense of life. Escaping with his comrades, he reflects that he has just gone through an adventure of the sort he had dreamed of as a boy, when he had heard the "sparse, enthralling tales" (232) spun by sea captains and soldiers. Now he has broken out of prison, has killed a man, and is fleeing for his life in a leaky boat. But the adventure does not seem really his, and he realizes why the tales he had listened to had seemed so crude:

> When you were living a tale you did not have time to color it as is should be colored—your mind stuck on odd useless trifles—the teeth of a man you struck—the feel of an iron bar—the

shape of a sail against the stars. Besides, in life you were hungry
and thirsty and had to make water—things which did not happen
in a tale, or, if they did, assumed heroic proportions.

(232-33)

Andrew feels cheated at the prospect of a world more drab
than he had imagined, but he faces up to it, as well as to the
pressing problem of regaining the safety of St. Augustine. Having
done so, though only after lighting a funeral pyre for the
Caterina he is half in love with and whom romantic convention
would have awarded him, he loses a final delusion, youth's
most cherished, "that life will come to a climax of thunder and
cease" (244). Yet he does not turn into a despairing fatalist,
the other side of the romantic coin: at the novel's end his
imagination lends charm to his reverie of a soldier's life in the
Revolutionary army.

Andrew's maturing, and indeed the whole novel, is given
another small dimension, partly satirical, partly historical, through
religion. The theme is peripheral to the central interests of the
story, but it has some significance. Andrew is a Scotch Presbyteri-
an whose baptismal water has been laced with the heady liquor
of the Enlightenment, though he does not analyze himself in
intellectual terms. In prison, however, he contrasts Sebastian's
Catholic faith that God is with them with his own feeling that
"God was something vague to pray to, for happiness or against
the approach of pain—something which might be there. . . . He
had never thought much about God except as a superior kind of
Archbishop of Canterbury who sat on a cloud and looked at
Papists sternly" (197). Reviewing his adventures, he fails to
discern any moral in them; mere accident has preserved him
and killed Mr. Cave, and he even wonders if he is better off
than Mr. Cave. For a moment he fears he is becoming a pagan;
then his ingrained Scotch Calvinism manifests itself and tells
him "it was not his business to question the schemes of God, but
to hold on dourly to a predestined path between damnation and
damnation, and distrust the vain speculations of the Egyptians"
(244). He only partially believes this ancestral voice, but it
sends him off to a sound night's sleep. The Colonial struggle
for freedom is what ultimately enlists his whole mind as well
as his body.

The religious theme reappears in the Roman Catholicism of

Sebastian's fellow Minorcans and even in two bizarre variations. One of these is Sebastian's supplication of an image of the Virgin with seven swords in her heart; this is Our Lady of Vengeance whose aid he seeks when Cave kills his pet monkey. The prayer is ultimately answered, but hardly through divine intervention. Equally futile is the learned Dr. Gentian's invocation of Baphomet from the fire. In an extraordinary passage full of esoteric references, this would-be Faustus offers a thousand souls—those of his workers—and his own for secret knowledge. But this survival of diabolism, Sebastian's ambiguous Catholicism, and Andrew's fading Protestantism serve to give historical plausibility to the novel.

Benét's own religious position emerges only in obscure imagery, as when he observes of his hero: "The cold brain of heaven, whose thought is a falling star between illusion and illusion, might properly regard his adolescent strugglings with befitting contempt but that task of scorn may, perhaps, be left to it" (180). Another image combines Christian and romantic symbolism: "The knowledge of good and evil had descended upon him at last, and he lay excruciated beneath it, like a harper crucified upon the strings of his own heart [sic]" (179-80).

Clearer meaning is conveyed by the symbol of the flower which gives the novel its title and constitutes another basis for asserting the work's superiority to the standard historical romance. Andrew first sees a bush of Spanish bayonet in a moonlit garden shortly after his arrival in Florida. It seems to him the most beautiful thing he has ever seen, with its single stalk of white petals rising from the green spikes of the plant "like a cold plume set upon a barbarous crest" (134). Benét points up the indigenous nature of the flower: "only in the hot night of the south could the ivory frond arise from among edged blades to challenge a tropic star" (134). As Andrew gazes on the enchanting flower, he feels himself on the verge of an immense discovery. Later, when he ecstatically kisses Sparta Gentian, he feels as if "the pointed blade of the Spanish bayonet had run him through and through with a golden thorn" (163). Later, after his shocking discovery of Sparta's corruption, the flower is associated with Caterina, whom he also loves, or is on the verge of loving, but does not understand. When she dies, he places a stalk of the plant on her breast, where it rests "like an order bestowed by the Moon" (239).

He thinks of Caterina when he is on a ship bound for New York, and the flower again rises before him, "incongruous, enchanted, pure" (257).

Spanish bayonet, with its primary qualities of beauty and danger, the beauty mysterious and ultimately unattainable, thus symbolizes the danger implicit in Andrew's two loves and indeed in his whole experience in Florida. On a deeper level the flower epitomizes the whole romantic conception—a lovely jeopardy which reality makes remote. This effective symbolism in the novel is furthered by an incident involving the night-blooming cereus and a flowered shawl which Sparta wears when she and Andrew go into the moonlit garden. Unfortunately, Benét failed to perceive that Sparta's family name, Gentian, demands symbolic values but does not afford them.

A final merit of the novel is that the situation in Florida duplicates in miniature that in the Northern colonies. In both instances a corrupt ruling family tyrannizes over masses of colonists and nurtures a still more ambitious imperialism. And in both instances a revolution takes place, resulting in the freedom of the colonials. In this fashion Benét manages to suggest the great historical event through the minor imagined one, but it cannot be said that he illuminates history.

Despite the over-all achievement of plausible characterization and background, and despite the infusion of some human, religious, and philosophical significance, the emphasis in *Spanish Bayonet* is on the melodramatic, at least to the extent that it overshadows the more serious claims of the novel. Written with evident care—"'I am praying it will be good,'" Benét told his wife[10]—with vivid and adequately detailed description of setting and character, rich and sensitive in style and only rarely lush, *Spanish Bayonet* is easily the best of his first four novels, if ultimately unsatisfactory. Reading it, a contemporary reviewer could with justice regard Benét as a novelist to watch.

V *James Shore's Daughter*

By the time *James Shore's Daughter* (1934) was published, such a reviewer might well have forgotten Benét the novelist in favor of Benét the poet and short story writer. *John Brown's Body* had brought him national prominence, as had some of his short fiction. In what proved to be the last of his novels, he sought to produce a work worthy of his new eminence. According to Fenton, "He was reaching for a wisdom and artistic purity which, save for *John Brown's Body*, he had not cultivated for ten years."[11] The aim cost him agonizing and exhausting struggles, but in the end he was dissatisfied. " 'Not what I want,' " he said, " 'but the best I can do. It should be a masterpiece in a small way—and it is not.' "[12] Benét was correct, but the novel is a fine one.

Although *James Shore's Daughter* runs to somewhat less than three hundred pages, it spans the Atlantic and the four decades from the end of the nineteenth century to the early 1930's. The two major themes are the international theme and the theme of American wealth. In preparation for the writing of the novel, Benét engaged in months of research, reading about the early 1900's and studying such books as Gustavus Myers' *Great American Fortunes*.[13] He also drew on his own extensive firsthand knowledge of the American rich, many of whom he knew. His familiarity with parts of Europe is also reflected in the novel. All in all, he employed his reading and his experience expertly and unobtrusively.

In one sense, the international theme in *James Shore's Daughter* is a means of providing another perspective on America. The narrator, Gareth Grant, is one of four children of an expatriate mother and a deceased artist-father. The mother and her children, whom she hopes will be geniuses, come to America after the death of the father in order to lend their cultivated guidance to the motherland—or so the mother envisions their mission as she returns to the New York society from which she sprang. At a party the ten-year-old Garry meets the eight-year-old Violet Shore, becomes a frequent visitor at the enormous Shore house on Sixty-second Street, and finds himself in love with her when his mother takes the family back to Europe.

This love, which Violet ultimately returns, generates the plot. But it cannot be fulfilled in marriage because Violet's father, the copper titan, arranges matters differently. He comes to like Garry; but, as he tells him when the Shores visit Paris some ten years later, Garry hasn't the chips to sit in on this particular poker game. His daughter—and his son—he says quietly, must have the best there is, in marriage as in everything else. Between the daughter and the father there is an unbreakable bond. As Garry puts it, ". . . you could feel a current running between them, as if they were copper, say, and the rest of the world were glass" (22). Shore, with apparent generosity, offers Garry an opportunity to prove himself in the industrial world and sends him off to study steel plants in France and Germany. The offer implies that Garry has a chance for Violet's hand. Governed by his sense of honor, he does not press his suit before he departs. When he returns to Paris, a letter from Violet informs him of her engagement to Charles Whipley Morton, the heir to an Eastern financial dynasty and a man who is all that Garry would like to be but feels he is not. Violet has already said to Garry of Charles, ". . . we both have money, so we needn't be afraid of each other at all. You don't know what that's like, especially to a girl'" (86).

Beaten in the most important game of all by Shore, the man from the West who always won, Garry, who had lusted to be a Richard Harding Davis hero, sets out to emulate Shore in the world of art. Twelve years after his rejection by Violet, he has achieved considerable success as an international art dealer and is still climbing. He resembles a prosperous seal and envisions an accompanying pomposity. When complacency leads him to forget why he has set out to climb, he thinks of James Shore and revives his motive. He has, he thinks, forever abandoned the society of great wealth, except to sell it works of art.

When Garry encounters Violet again, this time in 1912 in Vienna, he finds her mature and more beautiful than ever. His love reawakens, and he realizes that "We were made for each other, but not for each other and the lives we lived, each other and the desires we had" (127). Violet has learned much as the wife of Charles Morton, most of it disillusioning. Now on her second visit to Europe, she finds her earlier impatience with it transformed; she likes it very much. Intuitively she associates Garry with Europe. Her husband—whom her father has come to dislike—is intermittently disloyal. The rest of the Morton family she dislikes as fussy people. Too many people, Violet tardily perceives, sacrifice living for safety. Safety is not enough for her, now that she lives the life of the rich, with their eternal shuttling between great houses and fine climates. But, Garry observes, "The Shores only battled for one thing, and that was power" (147).

Violet and Garry, after increasingly intimate talks, establish a mutual sympathy and understanding that make a passionate climax almost inevitable. Yet their motives run too mixed, their lives have too long flowed in separate channels. Their act of love betrays them both, for they do not commit it with their essential selves for the essential self of the other. Vengeance and comfort are involved, and the delight passes too swiftly. Garry pleads with Violet to divorce her husband, but his beseeching lacks conviction. Then for a while he implores her to have a child by him, but she sensibly refuses, partly because "'it wouldn't be fair'" (158). Their liaison continues without spontaneity or true passion until the death of Violet's father brings to her a sense of the wrongness of their affair and to Garry a new realization of the money and the power that separate them. Now he possesses his own sense of power, and she will return to America and rule her husband and his family.

James Shore dies on the eve of World War I, and his epoch ends with him. Garry, who resumes his narrative in 1919, tells in brief retrospect of his service as an orderly sergeant in the British medical corps. His experiences have been grim, but the death of his beloved brother Carlo, his loss of interest and moral principles in his art business, and the near-collapse of his marriage are personal manifestations of the delayed postwar disintegration. The period is one of growing crisis for him. The loss of his brother wounds most deeply, because he had loved Carlo most deeply; because Carlo died after years of tuberculosis; because his tubercular wife had died earlier; and because he had been a fine writer and a great man—great, we may infer, in Garry's eyes, because Carlo had created art while Garry sold it.

The war has arrested the scheme of Garry and his partners to create what one of the latter called "a bloody Trust out of Art" (181). Sir Hugo Isaacstein, the brilliant merchant whom Garry admired and respected and who combined mercantile astuteness with a dream of making art integral with civilization, had worked on a project for ten years to produce cheap but beautiful, well-made things for everyday use. But Sir Hugo's two sons have been killed within a week of each other during the war, and he has lost interest in living. Garry reorganizes his own firm's London gallery but he has lost the knack of success. He becomes increasingly absorbed in making money to expiate his guilt over neglecting his family. Finally he sails for America to carry out a half-fraudulent business deal.

Benét fails to make wholly clear the reasons for the growing alienation between Garry and his wife Caroline, though the war has been the primary cause. Garry's motive in marrying her remains obscure, but she had married hoping for love. Her love had been gentle and natural, "something to be possessed in peace." In the beginning Garry had felt a strong drive to cherish and protect her, but this impulse had been insufficient for their happiness. In time it might have been enough, but the war came. It cost Caroline her two brothers, a loss which struck fear into her and made her guard herself against any further loss of a loved one.

Grant's six-week visit to America becomes a pilgrimage through which the meaning of the past becomes clearer to him, and he finds new directions for his life. His initial intoxication on returning to New York, the splendid and barbarous city that the James Shores had built, fades as he observes everywhere the bland standardization of the then commencing Harding-Coolidge era. The Shore mansion is being torn down to make way for a hotel, and the Shores have been succeeded by multitudinous bright young men of business.

Garry returns to the maternal family home in New England, inquires whether the local clay might be good for pottery, and wonders what the family had lost when it lost its way in the wilderness. Returning to New York and sitting in a speakeasy, Garry broods over his age—forty-two—and his life up to this point. He has done many inconsequential things; he is neither an artist nor a businessman, neither American nor European. "I had lost something in youth and made money instead" (223-24), he tells himself. Now he is going downhill. For a while he contemplates suicide. There is no way out of the speakeasy, he thinks, because there is no significance in his life.

The walls which enclose him in this symbolic prison fall away to release him in a room in which he talks to Violet for the last time. She feels the need to confide in him again and to escape the unremitting hurry that keeps her from saying all that should be said. She reveals that after their affair she had hated him and then herself. Now both the hates are over, but she still fails to see how love can be taken lightly. Love is cruel, she says; it is frightening to submerge oneself in another person. There should be another choice in life.

Garry reflects: this is a last, passionate outburst of that nature which had deserved to be owned by a man of greatness and splendor and instead had been possessed only by Charles Morton and himself. He is on the verge of consoling her with the thought that, though it is too late for love, it is not too late for the rest of life. But Violet's mood shifts, and she is repossessed by the values of the life she has chosen. She shows herself once again James Shore's daughter, proud of having forced her husband to do the big things, proud of her father. It is men like him who make the country, not the "cranks," she asserts.

As she says this, Garry realizes that he no longer believes in Jim Shore and what he represented. Garry still respects a certain quality in him, perhaps the quality of strong leadership. But already this quality has become anachronistic; the James Shores have been succeeded by the "imitation gentlemen and paper Napoleons." But Violet knew only the doctrine of the titans. Of this doctrine and all the ways in which his homage to it has warped him, Garry now is free.

Walking back to his hotel, he attains a further insight. He has always misjudged Violet Shore because he had loved her when he was a boy. He had both worshipped her and hated her, but she deserved neither, for she was merely a woman, "briefly alive on an inexplicable planet and bound to betray and be betrayed" (249). This humane perception humanizes Garry. He decides to abandon his dubious mission, his adventurer's life. He has just one responsibility—to his wife and children. It may be too late to carry it out, but he will try, for this enterprise is human. He gets out his revolver, a stupid thing, he sees, that cannot even end life. "Life went on forever and ever, in acts, in words, in memory, in the strangely compounded flesh. The one unpardonable sin was to perish, still in the flesh" (250). Then he laughs at his own pomposity and his petty defiance of man's fate—another act that humanizes him.

The brief postlude, set in the early years of the Depression, records Garry's reconciliation with his wife and his final inquiry into the nature of James Shore. His return to America and his setting up a small but excellent pottery are the concomitants of his reunion with his wife. Thus the cycle begun by his parents when they went to Europe in search of a richer cultural life is completed when the son and his wife find roots and a creative life at Maremmah, Garry's maternal home. Here he is content, and his wife, who must live close to the earth, is able to tear down the barrier of fear that had grown up between them.

On a business trip to California in 1933, Garry stops off at Gunflint, the Rocky Mountain town where Shore had begun the building of American Copper, where he had married, and where his daughter was born. Grant envisions the crude, tough mining town where Shore must have been wholly at one with his environment. Grant has always thought of Shore as the ruler of the metal, but now he understands that the metal had ruled him, driving him east across the continent and then to his death in Europe. The copper money had destroyed his son Aleck, making him a weakling, so that the father had had to leave the bulk of his fortune to establish a foundation. The money had not destroyed Violet, but it had become a part of her, making her assert her mastery over the Mortons. The fate of the Mortons was symbolic. They had been given the control of the nation— "and firmly, pompously, and almost automatically they had thrown it out of the window to land forty stories down" (261). Now there are many men in the streets without work.

Sitting in the home of an eager young copper-company executive rebellious against the Eastern management's apathy, Garry looks out over the valley and ponders the end of James Shore's time. He recalls Goethe sitting by the Prussian campfires at Valmy on the eve of the Napoleonic era and writing that he had witnessed the beginning of a new world. Life is difficult when one world ends and another begins, Garry observes. The builders of modern industrial America had thought their world stable and completed; but it had not even begun.

Nothing in this thoughtful novel is badly done, most things in it are well done, and a few things are brilliantly done. The novel's moderate length demands that Benét convey the essence of a period through carefully selected details of costume, setting, and social history, and through representative characters; and, for the most part, he has done this. Such minor elements as the conception of America which the Europeanized Grant children have acquired by reading *St. Nicholas*, the best-known children's magazine of the time, serve a double purpose—in this instance, that of suggesting simultaneously the prevailing "official" and spurious idealism of the nation during the late nineteenth century and the naïveté of the Grant youngsters. The European episodes do not consistently embody such deftly handled background material, but their level remains high.

The characters who serve to develop variations on the principal themes or who help to convey the flavor of their time are mostly drawn with remarkable vividness and economy. Memorable are some of the older persons: Garry's fading genteel cousin, who had devoted his life to the strange thing known as society; Violet's pathetic, senile Aunt Amy; and Grant's indomitable Victorian mother, author of the highly successful *Jaunty Heart* series of guide books, who at eighty-three writes a Victorian novel so out of date that it bursts on the literary scene like a radical new departure. In the early chapters Benét performs the difficult feat of making children act, think, and talk like plausible individuals. Some of the minor characters, however, such as Dickie De Saugres—the young French aristocrat and suitor of Violet, who is unpleasantly reminiscent of Hugues Parette—and Richards, the Cockney aesthete, fail to establish their fictional identities. More serious—since Garry regards him as a great man—is the hazy characterization of his brother Carlo.

Standing out vividly in front of these bas-relief figures are several other subordinate characters. Allen Barker, Shore's trained fox terrier, secretary, and bright young college graduate with a profound belief in business based solely on his reading, exemplifies the grey-flannel-suited young executive of the postwar generation. Benét sketches him with good-humored satirical strokes. Elsa Sunding, Shore's strong-minded, efficient nurse, late in the novel reveals her youthful lusts for wealth and power that she has long since buried under her Scandinavian coolness. Benét does a brilliant job of suggesting the just-beneath-the-surface tensions of this imposing but admirable woman. Her background as an immigrant and her seeking what Shore attained link her neatly to the central theme of the novel, and her adult rejection of wealth gives her authority as a critic of the man who is in her care.

Benét also manages to suggest with remarkable economy the contained power of James Shore, an achievement upon which the success of the entire novel depends. Shore's ruthlessness emerges with striking effect because of his quietness, his Western laconicism. Receiving a coded telegram in Paris, he sighs and comments, " 'Well, that puts McCuan out of business. I've been gunning for him a long time, but now that he's done with, I almost miss the man' " (68). When Grant asks why he was gunning for McCuan, Shore answers, " 'Oh, he thought he had me in a corner about six years ago. . . . But, as things turned out,

he didn't. You know, Colonel, a man like that is a good deal
of a nuisance. If you haven't got chips, there's no point sitting
in the game.'" In the same matter-of-fact manner he informs
Garry that he lacks the chips to sit in the game for his daughter's
hand; and just as coolly he deals Garry out.

Although Shore's power over others is demonstrated most
importantly in the domination he establishes over his daughter
and over Garry, it is his direct words and actions and Benét's
comments on them that register. Slowly dying, Shore orders
dozens of books, most of them classics. He does not read them
but seems to draw strength from merely owning them. "He had
them all under contract, so to speak, from Plato to Brann, and,
any time he chose, they would rise and deliver the goods" (143).
On his deathbed he says, "'My name's Jim Shore and I'm running
this'" (170). Yet Benét endows the man with a touch of playful
humor, with a thoughtful interest in the Cathedral of Chartres,
and with something veined in his character that remains Shore's
secret.

The first-person narrative technique raises problems of characterization that Benét does not completely solve. We learn
a good deal about Gareth Grant but not enough for him to
be the character Benét's high aim requires. The retrospective
technique unavoidably levies a tax in plausibility and immediacy
of effect; a fictional character cannot describe himself with
complete accuracy, particularly when he attempts to recall forty
or fifty years of his life; and the long backward look from the
vantage point of maturity must to some extent modify the
sharpness of reaction to life as it unfolds and tend toward a
unified point of view. In this way suspense is lessened. Through
the other characters Benét occasionally provides direct comments
on Garry's appearance or state of mind, but these are inadequate
to bring him sharply into focus at all times. Nevertheless Garry
is sufficiently sensitive and analytical for his role as seeker and
commentator, and his changing relationship with Violet Shore
is charged with considerable interest. She, however, also is rather
diffuse in outline; Garry asserts that he sees her finally as mortal
woman, but she lacks sufficient vivacity in her own right. Her
attitudes somehow remain a bit detached from her actions,
speech, and person. Benét, surprisingly, does not create his
characters physically. His keen awareness of color and texture
and physical form is translated into lively descriptions of settings,

but he does not employ it to give his men and women physical presences, accents, and mannerisms of their own.

Benét, according to his biographer, felt that the structure of *James Shore's Daughter* was not so good as it might have been,[14] but there are none of the blind alleys, wayward passages, or imbalances that mar his early novels. In fact, he handles very skillfully the complexities arising from the multiple task of catching the flavor and essence of an epoch on both sides of the Atlantic, of taking his protagonists through half or more of their lives, and of bringing in a large enough cast of characters to suggest various aspects of the era and even something of the baffling inconsistencies of life. The basic structure is a conventional division into five parts, but each covers a shorter period of a few months or years and represents a larger segment of the epoch—and the movements back and forth across the Atlantic are well timed.

Stylistically the novel, easily Benét's best, is intrinsically excellent. Only once does he lapse into the exaggerated romantic imagery that enfeebles the style of his earlier novels: when speaking of the lovers, he refers to "the barbarian voices, under the Roman accent, remembering, in ecstasy or anguish, neither Jove nor Venus, but the gods of desert and forest, the gods called Wind and Knife" (155). Nearly always in *James Shore's Daughter* Benét writes with concentrated force in a manner shorn of such fuzz. A few times his narrator becomes sententious; but, for the most part, he tells his story without embellishment. Now and then Benét seems to be so fearful of stating the obvious that his meaning is obscured; but clarity, compactness, and sensitivity predominate.

A number of pages in the novel stand out for their stylistic excellence or technique. In the latter category is an episode in which the young Garry, recalling pictures of the artist father he had not known, sees his lineaments subtly altered yet subtly unchanged in his clergyman uncle; the perception is half pathetic, half ironic. A score of passages are brilliantly satiric in various shades of that mode, ranging from the gentler though ample exposure of Garry's mother's triumphant feminism to the bulls-eyes on the rich: "Aleck always had to touch things before he could feel strong" (28). The plutocracy of the 1890's is scored in the summing up of New York conversation: "Democracy was a wonderful thing—it let all sorts of people get as rich as they wanted, and then you found out they were quite nice people after all" (23).

Benét's omnipresent sense of the disparity between what is and what ought to be can even deepen into stark elegy. Looking at his aging mother and her aging second husband, Garry is struck with the realization that they are solicitous of each other because there is no one else to look after them: "There was no one because each, by now, by the mere process of life, had become irreplaceable to the other, not only as a person but a custom, an echo, a bundle of memories. For memory is the end and beginning, it outwears beauty and splendor, it endures beyond sympathy and wit. And at the last we are glad to seek out our oldest enemy and talk to him of the things we have both known" (195-96). A sense of time's passing weaves through the novel, now sad, now asserting the urgent reality of the present.

In the days of their childish love, Violet Shore and Gareth Grant dream of their life together when they are grown up. They will live in the Rocky Mountains and be trappers. Amid the black mountains and the wild grass pastures, the snow and the streams, they will collect their rich pelts. In the dark night, with the snow heavy on the roof, the Indians will gather. Looking back on this dream, the grown-up Grant muses that the dream seems so vivid that it must have been real. All Americans, even the city-born, he thinks, have the nostalgia for the frontier; the sickness, even, he calls it. "It's a different curse from Europe's and a different fate" (28).

James Shore's Daughter in important ways is a novel about the frontier and the America that came after the closing of the frontier, with its enormous problem of mastering the wealth and power that men had wrested from the frontier. It is a novel rich with American meaning—even for today. Freedom means responsibility, and the individual cannot subordinate himself to things, or to the past. So stated, the meaning becomes a mere moral, but the terms that define it in the novel are complex and mature. *James Shore's Daughter* is, as Benét knew, not a masterpiece; it lacks the uniqueness, the consistent perfection or near-perfection of a masterpiece. It is what Benét would perhaps have been satisfied with: an honorable end to his otherwise disappointing novels, and a story that still merits appreciative readers.

CHAPTER 4

The Short Stories:
From Wholesaling to Artistry

*"Dear God, if there is a God, let
somebody be reading my three short
stories, sometime—somebody who isn't
a Ph.D. with a thesis."*

THE HISTORY of Benét's short-story writing is a record of
struggle with three adversaries: his innate preference for the
freedoms of poetry rather than the restrictions of short fiction;
the exigency of earning a living largely through marketable
stories; and the folly of magazine editors. The editors he with-
stood when to yield meant selling a principle; the substantial
income he needed he eventually attained; and the mastery of
the form he achieved after a prolonged struggle.

"'The short story,'" Benét admitted, "'was never exactly my
forte.'"[1] His biographer observes that creating his finer short
stories was a punishing process for Benét, imposing great psychic
and physical tension.[2] Even the commercial product did not
come easily. "'Finished another short story today,'" he reported
to his wife in 1921, "'a very short one, thank God, only 4,000
words. I tried to copy Millay-Boyd in it and rather produced
the effect of an elephant trying to walk the tightrope—I am not
at my best in the flippant sentimental.'"[3]

Perhaps because of his deep-seated uneasiness with and even
distaste for the short story, Benét did not experiment in its form.
In his best work, however, he gave to the traditional structure
an easy balance, an unobtrusive precision, and a finish that
reveal nothing of his travail in its composition. Despite his
choice of conventional form, he was characteristically undogmatic
about the form of the short story; he remarked that Edward

O'Brien, editor of the annual collections of the best American short stories, was " 'as prejudiced in favor of the formula formless story as the big-magazine-editor of 1925 was prejudiced against it.' "4 Benét found the older structure with a definite beginning, middle, and end—as practiced by Poe, by Henry James, or, in more leisurely fashion, by Washington Irving—more suitable for his own purposes than the Chekhovian moment-of-insight tale, as practiced in America by Sherwood Anderson. Benét came to employ the old device of a narrator in many of his stories, and he did so skillfully, making effective use of the greater immediacy, rapport with the reader, and interesting self-revelation or concealment which this point of view affords; but he did no pioneering in the form of the short story.

The scores of Benét stories that appeared in second- or third-rate mass circulation magazines during the 1920's and with less frequency during the 1930's attest to the degree to which he had to merchandise his creativity. As usual, he knew exactly what he was doing. He described one of his concoctions, written to help finance a year in Paris for the writing of *John Brown's Body*, as " 'a dear little candy-laxative of a tale about a sweet little girl named Sally . . . I do not see how it can fail to sell—it is so cheap!' "5 On another occasion he referred sardonically to " 'one of my celebrated, bright, gay stories of gay, bright, dumb young people.' "6 His bitterness, according to Fenton, was basically directed at the inflexible narrowness of the editors of the popular magazines which alone could pay him the money he needed. When the editor of the *Saturday Evening Post* asked Benét to alter the figure of investment broker Lane Parrington in "Schooner Fairchild's Class" so as not to make him such a stuffy representative of conservatism, Benét refused. He wrote his agent that " 'if you have to class-angle a story for the *Post* as you'd have to for the New Masses, only in reverse—there's no point in my trying to write for them. I can't work that way.' "7 Benét took this stand at a time when the *Post* had been paying him $1,250 a story.

Benét sought sometime during the mid-1920's to reconcile his artistic conscience with his financial needs by writing fiction stamped with his own originality and excellence yet possessed of wide popular appeal. He achieved this reconciliation by taking familiar materials from American history and folklore and mixing them with the bright colors of his imagination. " 'We have our

own folk-gods and giants and figures of earth in this country,' "
Benét once remarked. " 'I wanted to write something about
them.' "[8] Out of his ambition sprang such fresh, fine tales as
the Daniel Webster group—"The Devil and Daniel Webster,"[9]
"Daniel Webster and the Sea Serpent,"[10] and "Daniel Webster
and the Ides of March"[11]—"Jacob and the Indians,"[12] "A Tooth
for Paul Revere,"[13] "Freedom's a Hard-Bought Thing,"[14] and
"Johnny Pye and the Fool-Killer."[15] Not so good a story as any
of these but notable as the earliest example of Benét's use of
American types and legends is "The Sobbin' Women."[16] Though
it owes something to the legend of the Sabine women, Benét
transformed the Roman story through the use of such characters
as the Oldest Inhabitant of a nineteenth-century small town,
a hedge parson, and the seven brothers with American folk-hero
qualities. Later Benét widened his historical themes to include
European and contemporary affairs. History in one phase or
another is the subject of his finest short stories, as it is of his
poetry.

I *Daniel Webster Tales*

The Daniel Webster tales had their genesis when Benét
discovered that Van Wyck Brooks had brought the statesman to
life in *The Flowering of New England*.[17] Benét continued to
read about Webster until he conceived of the first of these
stories. In Webster, as Fenton has pointed out, Benét found an
ideal folk-hero, "ambiguous enough for productive characterization, less remotely sacred and frozen than Lincoln, majestic in
his strengths and weaknesses, national in his values."[18] That
the first Webster story touched historic and cultural affections
deep in the American mind is indicated by its immense success.
Published in the *Saturday Evening Post* in 1936, "The Devil and
Daniel Webster" gave Benét national recognition unequaled in
this period by any other American writer of his importance,
though similar in warmth to that accorded earlier to Irving and
Longfellow.[19]

The story's success prompted Benét to explain his intention
in writing it: " 'It's always seemed to me . . . that legends and
yarns and folktales are as much a part of the real history of a
country as proclamations and provisos and constitutional amend-
ments. . . . 'The Devil and Daniel Webster' is an attempt at
telling such a legend. . . . I couldn't help trying to show him

in terms of American legend; I couldn't help wondering what would happen if a man like that ever came to grips with the Devil—and not an imported Devil, either, but a genuine, home-grown product, Mr. Scratch.' "[20]

As Benét pointed out, Webster was most famed for his matchless oratorical powers; consequently, he would have to meet the Devil in an oratorical contest and defeat him.[21] The conflict between the Powers of Darkness and the powers of an American statesman has irresistible national appeal, and Benét had the shrewdness to add to the story not only regional humorous touches but universal human significance. The story's several thematic elements and wide range of tone, from the prevailing broad Yankee humor to the notes of pathos and even nobility, are combined in a superlative tale that comes to far more than humorous fantasy: it is a classic American fable.

This distinction is achieved in part through Benét's deft blending of the New England vernacular of his narrator, who is given only a regional identity, with subtler effects drawn from Benét's literary resources. The result is that the authentic ring of Yankee speech is enriched by semipoetic rhythms and imagery. Benét's imagination and regional and historical knowledge furnished the detail that helps give the story its sustained interest. Dan'l's ram Goliath, with his horn curled like a morning-glory vine; the tiny lost soul of Miser Stevens, carried in Mr. Scratch's handkerchief; the terrible hell's jury of American sinners that sits in judgment on Jabez Stone—these do their part to raise the story to its high level. Benét gains novelty by including on the jury such little-known figures from American history as Simon Girty, the renegade, and the Reverend John Smeet, the dainty strangler. The too-obvious choice of Benedict Arnold is cleverly avoided with the Devil's cryptic statement that Arnold is engaged in other business. The narrator's terminal comment that the Devil has never been seen again in New Hampshire, though he can't say anything about Massachusetts or Vermont, returns the story to the register of Yankee humor and state pride and saves it from over-serious moralizing.

The moral is at the story's core, however, and its meaning is drawn from the essence of American history. From one point of view "The Devil and Daniel Webster" is a reworking in American terms of the biblical story of Job and the Faust legend. Jabez (the name is suggestive) Stone, unlike Job, in the beginning is a poor man (and "not a bad man") whose poverty is caused by bad luck. His troubles, particularly with his farm, finally make him so desperate that he sells his soul to the Devil, not for power, like the German, but for the American dream of prosperity. The soul of Jabez is contested for, not by God and the Devil, but by an American demigod and Mr. Scratch. Jabez, unlike Faust, can be saved, for the genius of America as embodied in Daniel Webster, uses reason and eloquence to awaken pity for another, even among the damned. Humane justice, not strict justice, is accomplished, since Jabez undeniably made his contract. When Daniel argues that the Devil is a foreign prince without power over an American citizen, the Devil slyly claims older citizenship than Webster himself. He was, the Devil says, present when the first wrong was done to the Indians, when the first slaver put out for the Congo. When Webster allows his opponent to select whatever judge and jury he wishes, so long as they are American, Judge Hathorne of the Salem witchcraft trials and a wicked dozen are summoned from hell—Americans all.

Webster miraculously wrings mercy from these stony unregenerates by reawakening their sense of manhood. He evokes simple joys of common life, the things good for any man, but things that can be enjoyed only under freedom. While conceding all the wrongs that have ever been committed in America, he shows that something new has been born here. Everyone has played a part in the process, even traitors. Jabez Stone is hard and mean, but he has good in him, and he is a man. Being a man is a sad thing, but it is a proud thing too, Webster demonstrates. Even in hell, a man can be recognized.

As he argues, Webster makes his plea for Jabez a plea for all men. It is also a plea for Dan'l himself: he has seen that the jurors are after him as well as Jabez and will get him if he fights them with their own weapons. Dan'l goes on to retell the story of all men with all their failures and deceptions and their long journeying. Only men can see the greatness of the journey. And their own manhood momentarily restored, the demon-jury finds for the defendant, deciding by the spirit rather than the letter of the law. Daniel Webster even lets the Devil go. He'll be around, again, at least in some of the United States, but he has been mastered by justice, by humanity, by the hero of the country that represents mankind's best hope. With these rich but neatly integrated increments of meaning Benét invests his legend with seriousness as high as his humor.

Benét did not equal this achievement in his other two Webster stories. In the sea-serpent tale, for instance, Benét creates another humorous myth but fails to weld it to a proportionate amount of national significance. And in a piece like "The Angel was a Yankee"[22] he attempts to capitalize cheaply on a New England stereotype, popular religion, and the epic showmanship of P. T. Barnum. A touch of poetry in the description of the angel and occasional bits of humorous character contrast are insufficient to overcome the commonplace style and obviousness of theme. More expert is "A Tooth for Paul Revere," in which Benét takes liberties with the famed story to make in fresh fashion the point that the American Revolution began when the common man, through whatever homely circumstances, joined the leaders in becoming involved in political issues.

II *Historical Realism*

Benét's gifts for re-creating history were sometimes channeled into realism with laudable results. His method in such stories as "The Die-Hard," "Jacob and the Indians," and "Freedom's a Hard-Bought Thing" was to imagine a figure representative of a phase of American history and to take him through experiences reflecting the essence of the period. This kind of story requires a central character who is typical yet sufficiently individualized or otherwise interesting enough to sustain the reader's attention.

Benét succeeded in making his hero in "Jacob and the Indians" a plausible young Jewish scholar whose adventures are not too improbable for eighteenth-century America. Immigrating to America from Germany in order to escape a plague and tyranny, he continues his studies but must spend his days peddling trinkets in Philadelphia. Falling in love with the lovely daughter of the wealthy merchant from whom he buys his merchandise, he learns that he is out-rivaled by an aggressive young Jew who is becoming rich through trade with the Indians. In jealous anger, Jacob resolves to go into the wilderness to prove himself the better trader. He seeks the help of another wealthy merchant who tells him he has come to Pennsylvania because of William

Penn's promise of freedom. The merchant talks cryptically of the promise of a new nation growing out of the wilderness but gives Jacob the help he needs.

Jacob goes into the wilderness with a Scottish trader who is obsessed with the idea that the Indians beyond the Western Mountains are the Ten Lost Tribes of Israel. They come to the Mississippi and see the endless country beyond it, but the Scotchman dies of an illness and Jacob is captured by the Shawnees. They begin to burn him at the stake but free him when his anger makes him behave with reckless courage. After living with them through the winter, he escapes and returns to Philadelphia with a load of furs and the scalp of his one-time hated rival, who has been killed by the Indians. He tells his merchant-sponsor of plans for new trading posts, but he cannot tell the merchant the full truth of his terrible experiences in the West, nor of the endless country he has seen. He is a changed man, he believes. The Jew tolerantly realizes that he must stand for all men in the new land, for his friend McCampbell, a Gentile, has died there.

This story skillfully weaves the staple American themes of tolerance, trade, the opening of the West, and the transformation of men's characters by the New World. The Jewish flavor of the story comes not only from the characters but from the unobtrusive inclusion of bits of Hebrew lore, customs, and learning. The narrator, Jacob's great-great-granddaughter, serves not only to provide a disarming, chatty opening but to make the Jewish elements seem more authentic. The disputes between Jacob and McCampbell over the latter's theory of the Ten Lost Tribes are amusing, but they also show a common love of learning and foreshadow the Jew's love for the Scot. The introduction of a dove-eyed granddaughter of the merchant at the story's end is unnecessary and is a too-neat balancing of accounts for Jacob, but there are no other major flaws. Not a great story, "Jacob and the Indians" is a good example of Benét's ability to incorporate a good deal of American history in brief compass and to give it the color of living reality.

A finer tale of the same sort, one which brought Benét the O. Henry Memorial Award for the best short story of 1940, is "Freedom's a Hard-Bought Thing."[23] The representative nature of the story is indicated by the many letters Benét received from descendants of escaped Negro slaves and from operators of the underground railway when the story was first published in the *Saturday Evening Post*.[24] The story acquires its impact from its thoroughgoing realism and powerfully developed moral. Once again Benét demonstrates his exceptional talent for catching the speech rhythms, the diction, and the point of view of a national or ethnic type. Here it is a Negress, presumably an old freed slave herself, telling children the story of Cue, born a plantation slave. The narrator's grammatical elisions, her use of dialectal and religious terms, and her sentence structure which immediately shifts to accommodate her emotional meaning are speech characteristics which identify her but do not get in the way of her story.

Cue grows up strong, proud, and willing, and is put to work in the plantation blacksmith shop. He likes his work and is content until his parents die in an epidemic. Their loss makes him begin to ask himself questions. He sees that their cabin is given to new slaves, and that all they have left is their burying ground. Finally he goes to consult Aunt Rachel, rumored to be a conjure woman. She diagnoses his trouble as freedom sickness— a big trouble. She tells him of the road that runs underground and of the way to find it. Cue runs away but is soon caught and whipped, though let off lightly because of his good record. He ponders the advice Aunt Rachel has given him, and even sets himself the task of learning to read, so that he may get some of the wisdom of the white folks. Finally he talks to a white man who tells him of freedom and of the underground railroad. But Cue is again barred from freedom on his second attempt to escape when he gives the last place on a boat to his girl Sukey. Marked as a runaway, he feels bitter toward Aunt Rachel; the burden of winning freedom is too heavy for him. But the crone tells him of the ancient freedom of her people and the long road ahead to freedom, and Cue knows that he is bound to be a witness for freedom. Sold to harsher owners, he knows suffering and cruelty. When at length he runs away a third time, he gets through to the underground railway; and, though constantly in jeopardy, he arrives in Canada. At first unable to realize his new condition, he finally gives himself a full name—John H. Cue—to signify his new identity as a free man.

The resemblance of this story to biblical parables accounts for much of its force. Cue's strength of body and mind makes him a symbol of all slaves who struggled for their freedom, and the speech patterns of his storyteller, as well as several direct invocations of the Lord, echo the King James Bible. The narrative of a whole people, implicit in the story, is made explicit in the racial memories of Aunt Rachel (whose name is appropriately drawn from the Old Testament). At the same time, Benét partially individualizes Cue and gives his story enough particulars to imbue it with a telling realism. Carefully selected details like the bubbling and chunking pot in Aunt Rachel's cabin are suggestive as well as realistic, and her advice to Cue to study the rabbit in the briar, the owl in the woods, and the star in the sky adds a touch of folk poetry. Benét's romanticism unnecessarily bestows another Sukey on Cue at the end, but the sentimentalism has some justification in its suggestion of the race's continuity under freedom. The story is virtually flawless.

III *Folklore and Fantasy*

Benét did not always stress fulfilled promise in his use of native materials, either for poetry or fiction. In "Johnny Pye and the Fool-Killer"[25] he employed folklore concerning the always lurking and invincible dispatcher of those who violate common sense—that is, everyone. The story illuminates a grim side of folk literature corresponding to a deep but subdued preoccupation of Benét's which emerged principally in some of his short poems.

Johnny Pye is the familiar literary type of the naïve youth who comes to wisdom through hard experience—in this instance, a good slice of American experience. An orphan in a small town, Johnny runs away from the miller and wife who adopt him, for their notion of the proper way to make a child better and brighter is to treat him like a fool. Already fearful of the legendary Fool-Killer, Johnny takes to the road when the miller tells him he's the most foolish boy he's ever seen. Apprenticeships with a quack herb doctor who makes the mistake of returning to a town, and with a merchant who is totally absorbed in joyless money-making, again put Johnny on the run to avoid similar follies. His gantlet takes him past an inventor of a perpetual motion machine, a drunken fiddler, brave but rash soldiers and Indians, a Republican congressman, a Democratic congressman, and a President of the United States; these last three are convinced of the omniscience of their parties.

Johnny again hears the steps of the Fool-Killer the night he wins the hand of the girl he loves, but he marries her anyway and accepts the President's appointment as postmaster in his home town. A happily married father, Johnny unexpectedly encounters the Fool-Killer—not the big man with a hickory stick he had imagined but an old scissors-grinder putting an edge on a scythe. It's Johnny's time, the Fool-Killer tells him; but when Johnny protests, the old man agrees to a postponement. In fact, he offers permanent reprieve—the first in history—if Johnny will answer one question: how a man can be a human being and not be a fool.

When he is past forty, Johnny, now a solid citizen, loses his eldest son through drowning. Mad with grief, he tries to fight the Fool-Killer when he sees him; but the old man evades him and reminds him that time passes, though it will not heal his grief, and that he must return to his wife and other children. With the passage of years, he acquires grandchildren but loses his wife. When he is ninety-two, Johnny meets the Fool-Killer, whom he has forgotten, for the last time. He remembers his question, however, and he has an answer, or at least a partial one. Though all men are fools, the brave and the wise and the clever make the world progress an inch now and then. But all types and qualities of men are mixed together; only a creature foolish by nature would have come out of the sea onto dry land or have been ejected from the Garden of Eden. But Johnny doesn't have much use for a man who hasn't been thought a fool by some who knew him.

His question answered, at least as well as Johnny can answer it, the Fool-Killer carries out his part of the agreement by offering eternal life. After thinking the matter over, Johnny declines on the grounds that his physical decay will continue unchanged. As the Fool-Killer puts it, he can hardly expect to be the same man at a hundred and eighty that he was at ninety. Moreover, Johnny reflects, his wife and friends have gone, and there'd be no one with real sense to talk to if he hung around until Judgment Day. Still, if he goes along with the Fool-Killer now, he wonders if he'll see his friends later, as some folks believe. The scissors-grinder can't tell him that, he says; he only goes so far. Johnny Pye leaves with him, content to go that distance.

Again in this tale Benét varies his style to suit his substance. Although he begins by addressing the reader directly—"You don't hear much about the Fool-Killer these days"—the yarn-spinner has no identity beyond this function. He is an anonymous voice from the anonymous folk, weaving fantasy and humor and wisdom from the stuff of a people's common experience. He tells his story plainly, directly and vividly, without fuss or moralizing or metaphysical speculation. The humor he conveys dead-pan, in the tradition of Mark Twain and Artemus Ward. The humor of the first part of his story, obvious but as telling as Ward's, roundly whacks American limitations and pretensions. Benét subtly accomplishes the shift into the graver part of his story with Johnny's discovery that the Fool-Killer is not the American bruiser of his imagination but the personification of Time in the guise of a familiar American figure. The theme of the story changes with Johnny's wise perception that folly is a part of all men, but *only* a part—and a humanizing one at that. His recognition of this truth is placed in the framework of the American conception of man as a creature with possibilities as well as limitations. But finally the storyteller's theme is human mortality; and quiet pathos, with a bit of transcendental hope, ends his tale.

Benét was by no means consistently successful with such material. "William Riley and the Fates,"[26] for example, is another fantasy attempting a humorous mixture of transcendental figures and American philosophizing, but its mode is commonplace and its meaning no deeper than that of a newsreel. "O'Halloran's Luck"[27] reveals expert craftsmanship, although it relies too heavily on familiar Irish types, human and fairy, to be ranked as one of Benét's best stories. "Doc Mellhorn and the Pearly Gates,"[28] while commendable for its thesis that doing good works in hell is preferable to doing nothing in heaven, remains superficial in its development and suffers from the sentimental clichés which compose the chief character. "The Minister's Books,"[29] though it grew out of Benét's research into frontier history,[30] has a startling thematic and stylistic resemblance to Nathaniel Hawthorne's tales of Puritan New England. Competently done, it is yet essentially imitative except in respect to Hawthorne's genius for endowing the natural and supernatural with manifold moral meaning. A quite different story with considerable imagination is "The King of the Cats."[31] In it Benét ingeniously adapted an old European legend to a modern American setting for social satire, as well as pure fun.

IV   *Science Fiction and A Dream of History*

These and other lesser stories mingling American themes with the fantastic or supernatural are overshadowed by a fine story of a sort which rarely ascends to the level of serious literature. "By the Waters of Babylon"[32] is science fiction in that it is set in the indeterminate future after a holocaust has destroyed American civilization. The story is prophetic in the best sense, in that it draws on the wisdom of the past to indicate the path of the future for civilization, while at the same time the evils of the nation are exposed. By the title Benét evokes the destruction of the Israelite nation and the lamentation of the survivors, and, more distantly, the warnings of the Old Testament prophets. His story's prophecies are likewise indirect and subtle, and more moving than a jeremiad.

Benét's narrator is the son of a priest of the Hill People who inhabit America when its name is no longer known or spoken. They are, so to speak, a post-American Indian nation at approximately the same stage of civilization as their pre-Columbian prototypes. In suggesting the nature of their culture, Benét relied on his intuitive sense of pre-Colonial America of the sixteenth century.[33] John and his people hold in awe the Dead Places and the gods who once inhabited them. Taboos surround the Dead Places but, guided by a dream and omens, John, who also wishes to be a priest, makes his way into the colossal ruins of New York. At night, sleeping in an apartment, he dreams of the city as it had been when inhabited by the innumerable restless gods who turned the night into day for their pleasure. Then he sees the fire fall from the sky, and witnesses the death of the gods. Waking perplexed in the morning, John goes into a room to find the mummified body of one of the gods who had stayed to watch the destruction of his city. There is wisdom in his face, and great sadness. But John sees that he had not lost his spirit. He knows him for a man, not a god. John and his people, the new men, must seek the wisdom and knowledge of the men who were there before them. Civilization must begin again.

In "By the Waters of Babylon" Benét again succeeds brilliantly in creating a narrator to develop his meaning: a noble savage made believable. The dignity, simplicity, and rhythm of John's language admirably mirror the state of culture of his people, and his primitive religion and virtues present a haunting contrast to the complexity and sophistication of the New Yorkers. His awe for the gods, then his pity for them, and finally his recognition of a spiritual greatness in at least some of them create a poignant sense of the tragedy of civilization. Benét astutely leaves the cause of the war unexplained; whatever it was, it could not justify the tragedy. And since throughout the story he creates the utmost sense of the reality of his narrator and his experiences, the story preaches with the eloquence of the sermons said to be in stones. "By the Waters of Babylon" is religious not only through the primitive rites and aspirations of the narrator, but fundamentally through Benét's reverence for civilization.

Similar in conception, though less noble a tale, is "As It was in the Beginning."[34] The biblical echo in the title summons up the history of the Israelites; Benét through his narrator recounts the exodus of the People of the Short Grass and their long quest for freedom. Oppressed by the injustice of the distant king who rules them, the People of the Short Grass rebel and make their way across the mountains, carrying the image of their god, Atli. They have chosen the indomitable dreamer Marco as their leader, their Old One, though he does not believe in Atli. After many hardships and deaths, they reach the still fairer land of the People Who Wear Bronze. The higher civilization of the Bronze People does not save their city nor their god from capture by the new arrivals.

When Marco dies, weary of the burdens of leadership, the tyrant Iron siezes power. He oppresses the Bronze People as well as his own people, and he embarks on wars of conquest until it becomes necessary to kill him. Char, the negotiator and the chess player, becomes the Old One and rules well. When he dies, his son succeeds him. With peace and wise leadership, the people prosper and their arts increase. Atli changes from a vindictive little god desiring sacrifice to a kind and stately god. The People of the Short Grass and the Bronze People become brothers. But Karn, the historian, sees that this is but the beginning. War is rumored; their one-time king may move against them. And a stranger, speaking an unknown tongue, has landed on their shores. Are there distant lands and new people? Some day the People of the Short Grass will know, for now they are men, with the freedom to choose. Their journey continues.

The meaning of the tale is stated at the outset: the freedom and fame of a people always exact a price, and the price changes. The moral is implicit in the American experience as well as the Israelite, though Benét skillfully avoids too close a parallel with either history. The People of the Short Grass have kinship too with the Indians of the Great Plains before the coming of the Europeans, and suggestions of other cultures appear from time to time in the story. Benét adds some details with no cultural connotations, as well as some universal elements like the developing conceptions of deity. The result is that his story is weighted with associations heightened by strangeness, like a dream in which familiar elements are rearranged in new and half-mysterious yet meaningful patterns. Too explicit a declaration of the story's meaning at the outset and at the conclusion weakens the poetry of this dream of history; and the confident conclusion, implying a steady march of civilization, does not rest solidly on the chronicle's record or the historian's personal experience. Yet Benét has registered effectively through indirect means his summing up of the historic lessons of freedom.

V *Transmuting European History*

Benét could also transmute specifically European history, ancient or modern, into a fine short story. "The Last of the Legions,"[35] published in 1937, is a superb tale of the decline of the Roman Empire. The shadow falls down fifteen centuries of history to darken the decade of the twentieth century in which Hitler's new barbarians stormed the gates of European civilization. The story exists in two phases of time: its past points to the ominous future of the reader contemporary with its publication. The post-World War II reader may see in it still another, even more terrifying, application.

Benét's narrator is a senior centurion with a proud legion, the Twentieth, the Valeria Victrix. It has held the northwest region of the Empire in Britain for 358 years, fighting off the Scots and the Northmen. Now it is being transferred to Gaul, and the post is turned over to British auxiliaries. The storyteller is a child of the camp, born in Britain, but a stalwart Roman, loyal to the core. At first the centurion is confident that the Twentieth will soon return, or will be replaced by another legion, but as he marches southeast towards a channel port, he sees increasingly ominous signs of imperial catastrophe. He has sat up all night persuading a young recruit in love with a girl in the town not to risk death by torture because of desertion, but the recruit, another child of the camp, disappears at the second halt. Half a dozen others also desert, but, after two are punished as examples, the desertions cease.

As the legion moves into the lovely, soft south of Britain, the master of a fine villa, fearful of the coming of the Northmen, attempts to bribe first the general and then the centurion to enable him to escape with the legion. Both refuse, but the centurion has a terrible vision of the fallen walls of the villa and of the naked barbarians huddling around a dim fire in the rain. Then he walks through a courtyard where orange trees grow and bright fish play in the pool. As the legion embarks, the narrator knows that, though the Twentieth will fight and will both win and lose, its time is over. Ahead lie the wide channel and the great darkness of Gaul.

The philosophical meaning of "The Last of the Legions" emerges largely through the conversations between the centurion and Agathocles, a Greek attached to the legion to keep its accounts. As a representative of a great culture now fallen into decadence, its vitality gone, as he acknowledges, the still-proud Greek makes ironic sallies against the Roman attitudes of his comrade. His cleverness provides a foil for the stolid and unimaginative centurion; Agathocles regards himself as a philosopher, seeking cause and effect. The deserter he sees as a soothsayer, prophesying by his flight the fall of the Empire. All Greeks are eaters of wind, the Roman retorts; but finally the Greek's words get under his skin, and he begins to observe things he would not otherwise have noticed. In the end he utters for the first time to Agathocles the name of Alaric the Goth, who is reported to be approaching Rome.

Various elements of the story exemplify the causes of Rome's decay—the centurion's limitations of mind and spirit, the use of torture to uphold military discipline, the inferior military prowess of the pacified peoples, the cultivated corruption of the rich and their great influence over the government, the remoteness from Rome of the outposts of Empire. Beyond these causes Agathocles adds a more searching though inconclusive commentary. He does not admire the Romans, but he concedes their greatness. Though they had nothing but an arch, a road, an army, and a law, they unified the world from East to West and gave it a common tongue. But now the spirit of destruction in man is outpacing the spirit of building, though the Greek does not know why. Men dream and build, and then their dream is shaken to pieces by the storm, not quickly, but over a long time. Then come the darkness and the howling peoples.

When the Roman reminds the Greek of his own state and law, Agathocles says his people could have kept them but they did not. They had Pericles; they shamed him. The shapers of civilization possess greatness and wisdom, but the people must recognize them and choose them. This story of Benét's, which has the sombre magnificence of black marble, is compact of wisdom and greatness in aesthetic form. High among its virtues is the subtle shift in the verbal style of the narrator from his initial matter-of-fact soldier's manner to a sweep and rhythm of language appropriate to his rising sense of imperial tragedy.

Benét in "Into Egypt"[36] dealt directly with an immediate twentieth-century tragedy of history, though he gave it a longer perspective, both historical and moral, from the viewpoint of Christianity. Written in December, 1939, after shocking news from Berlin of the Nazi slaughter of the Jews,[37] the story presents, through the screen of rationalizations of a young Nazi lieutenant, the exodus from Hitler's Germany. The highly sensational material becomes one of the memorable pieces of anti-Nazi literature through Benét's adroit handling, and until the end it is one of the best. It is made so chiefly by Benét's delineation of the young officer, with his correct official attitudes, his borrowed belief that only if the troublesome Accursed People are driven from the country can one become a whole man, solid and virile. The lieutenant is sentimental, too, dreaming of marriage and of Christmas in the South where he grew up. Watching the wailing refugees stream past the crossroads checking-point over which he has command, the lieutenant perceives that the Jews (though he does not use the term) contradict the official propaganda, for they differ radically among themselves in person, in station, and in manner. However, his function is not to think about such matters but to do his duty as an officer. Yet when a final straggling little family comes along with a donkey, he allows them to keep the animal for the rest of their journey rather than turn in a ridiculous report of one confiscated donkey.

At this point the perceptive reader will recognize the Holy

Family; others will wait until the lieutenant's revelation that the child's hands were pierced. Whatever one's acuity, the shock is excessive. The realistic portrait of the young Nazi and the collective portrait of the Jews suffice to represent the terrible moral exigency of the time. An orderly's observation that civilians are sheep almost suffices to evoke the pastoral Christ; the lieutenant's Christmas reverie almost overstates the theme, though there is ample historical evidence of such a dichotomy in the Nazi mind. To superimpose, however expertly, the supernatural, surcharged symbols of Christianity on realistic twentieth-century portraiture seems a virtuoso trick rather than the reflection of Benét's outraged moral sensibilities, which it doubtless was in origin.

"The Blood of the Martyrs,"[38] a story written a few years earlier, moves strictly within the confines of realism, except that its title draws upon Christian hagiography. Its hero is again a victim of the Nazis, though they are not so identified. Professor Malzius, a selfless man of science, is dedicated to the search for truth in his field, biochemistry. World famous as a scientist, he has been imprisoned because of his refusal to furnish information about the political activities of his students. Offered the presidency of a national academy of science in exchange for open advocacy of the militant doctrines of the new state, the professor discards his lifelong belief that politics is none of his concern. His defiance costs him his life. The quest for truth in biochemistry, he comes to understand, is but an aspect of the larger search. The story is ably done but undistinguished; it is not quite capable of rising above its somewhat familiar materials and characterization.

"The Curfew Tolls"[39] takes complete liberty with history for the purpose of making the point that greatness is the handmaiden of chance and circumstance. Benét makes his incontestable point through the flamboyant example of Napoleon Bonaparte. What if the Corsican had been born thirty years earlier, had staked everything on getting to India to fight the English, had been captured in the last battle of the campaign? Benét imagines him as an obscure major of fifty-two, retired on half pay, and eaten with bitterness at the wasting of his genius in captivity and garrison duty. Contrived though the story is, Benét manages to give it vitality by catching precisely the mixture of genius and rascality that Napoleon was. The epistolary form of the story, a variation on Benét's usual first-person narration, presents Bonaparte through the eyes of a retired British general who encounters him at a French watering spot and who adds some amusing ironies and significant contrasts in national character.

In "The Bishop's Beggar,"[40] Benét subordinated history to character and plot without reducing history to mere background and color. With the story set in Renaissance Italy, Benét at the outset links the bishop with his time—one stirring with the revival of learning and turning men to the pursuits of this world rather than the next. Thwarted in his earlier ambitions, the bishop has entered the church as another arena in which fame may be won. Handsome, young, clever, he is worshiped by the people of his diocese, yet a vague disquiet troubles him. It is succeeded by a specific and ever-increasing burden when his carriage, through no fault of the bishop, cripples a young boy. The bishop assumes responsibility for the lad and, against his will, yields to the boy's ambition to become the bishop's beggar. This worldly aspiration is the summit of the attainable for the cripple, a fact not lost on his protector. The fastidious prelate dislikes beggars, but he suffers Luigi with outward patience. The new man of the Renaissance finds that his vainer interests clash with the spiritual duty laid upon him by his church.

This central conflict generates the high interest of the story. Benét traces with exactitude the bishop's acquisition of knowledge not of the classics but of the world of the beggars, the world of the poor. Under the elegant surface of the city of Remo lie incredible suffering and sin. Little by little these evils engage the energies of the bishop and draw him from his lordly pursuits. As the years pass, he is weaned from his ambition to attain the highest offices in the church and is nourished by the hope of easing the troubles of his people. At length his dedication attracts the notice of the Holy Father, and he is offered a cardinal's hat in a diocese just outside Rome. He refuses because his beggar is eager for his own ascent on the steps of a new cathedral; the bishop turns down the promotion to save Luigi's soul.

What saves the story from being a sentimental religious romance is the sharp realism with which Benét delineates Luigi and the bishop. On the verge of death, the beggar reveals his long hatred of his benefactor. Though he has confessed every other sin to him, he has never revealed his worst one: the ambition which has sustained him is the hope of seeing the bishop abandon his diocese and thus lose his soul. Luigi's ultimate love for the bishop is made plausible because his hate has never been pure, just as the bishop's eventual salvation is made credible by Benét's early mention of his questioning tendency.

Luigi's dying curiosity as to whether it is drafty on the steps of heaven is a stroke not wholly offset by Benét's terminal comment on the boy's arrogance, but the prevailing mature ironies and objective narration, coupled with the firm setting in history, combine to make this one of Benét's finest stories. The rising fascination of the story attains its climax in an ingeniously conceived episode that forms a logical prelude to the final understanding between the protagonists. Superficially the story seems uncharacteristic of Benét—a non-Catholic and probably an agnostic—in its affirmation of traditional religious values over Renaissance worldliness, but the story should not be read as a complete statement of his position on the issue. In any event, the spiritual essence of the story, the uncondescending, humane concern with the dispossessed, is typical of Benét.

VI *Contemporary Life*

Benét's stories of contemporary life are collectively somewhat inferior to his tales woven from the stuffs of fantasy and history, and only one of them has the stature of "The Bishop's Beggar." In addition to the boy-girl fluff and the antitotalitarian stories, Benét attempted some serious studies of the generation he knew intimately. He touches on various facets of the time; but, for one reason or another, few of these tales are first-rate. "Schooner Fairchild's Class"[41] has the laudable intention of pointing out how much lifetime passage on the Ivy League-Wall Street circuit impoverishes life; but the broker who comes to realize the extent of his stuffiness is too much of a straw-hat man to arouse much sympathy, and his change of philosophy is unconvincing. His foil, the engaging university class-clown, is too fragile a figure to be an effective counterweight. Benét does widen the range of his story by introducing a young couple, the broker's son and the clown's daughter, who represent the hopeful future; but they also are too familiar fictional characters to lend the story distinction.

Other stories, though lacking in depth and technical superiority, develop Benét's praiseworthy concern for the good life not practiced by his generation. One of the better ones in this category is "Everybody Was Very Nice."[42] In this satire, in the manner of Ring Lardner or Sinclair Lewis but with the targets shifted to the upper-middle class range, Benét once more relies on the technique of unconscious self-revelation, and with telling results. The universal blandness of manners that lubricate but do not end the grinding moral dislocations of modern divorce, Benét attributes to the advanced belief of the wealthy in romance as a supreme value. "The Story About the Anteater"[43] sums up the eternal husband's joke which stretches the marriage bond to the breaking point but which finally becomes a symbol of a wife's mature contentment. This story, with its facile resolution, is perilously close to run-of-the-washer fiction. "Too Early Spring"[44] contrasts the innocence of teen-agers with the guilty sexual consciences of the adults whose accusations twist the lives of a boy and a girl. The story instances Benét's customary attitude of mixed common sense and faith regarding young people, but the contrasts are obvious and the climax implausible.

The war between successive generations is explored more deeply, even memorably, in "The Prodigal Children,"[45] with the two world wars furnishing some intricate patterns of personal tensions. Benét avoids an easy distribution of virtues and vices according to date of birth; he portrays the artistic elite of his own generation with keen perception of the particular mixture that distinguished it. The story's opening in a little New England restaurant "discovered" by an alert couple satirizes the self-conscious savoring of good food and the sophisticated appreciation of the quaint and undiscovered that marked the generation which made World War I. Now it is 1942, and the young red-headed girl with the group bitterly tells herself that these are the people who have got the world in a mess that she and her ensign and their generation will have to straighten out. Naïve, moral, earnest, the girl makes her blunt judgments with the rebellious intolerance of the young. Yet she has her justification: she has grown up among the wonderful people, who divorce so easily, like her own parents. And now she must drive her young man to the train and come back through the blackout.

Returning to the party somewhat shaken after her long drive in the darkness, she is taken in charge by Harry Crandall, the writer. He, having turned to writing propaganda (as Benét himself did), knows that he may ruin his professional reputation. Yet it is his war; he knows not only that his generation is in some sense responsible for it but that freedom is at stake. He perceives the limitations of himself and his friends and colleagues; but they have their values too. They had zest for life, and they sought and found some of the good things in it—fine food and wine, good talk, and freedom, including the freedom to be themselves. They had gone on a queer adventure which after twenty years had brought them back to things they had forgotten and which they must now fight for; they are the prodigals. Crandall has a generous grasp of people's motives and values and an understanding of the girl's point of view which, so to speak, provide something of an apology for Benét's generation. Whatever their shortcomings, they seized life with both hands, he tells himself, as he stands in the night with the girl, who has regained her healthy confidence in the future which she will help make. Benét never distilled more of his time into any of his writings than he did in "The Prodigal Children": his insights and his breadth and depth of understanding make this story worthy of inclusion with the best of Hemingway's and Fitzgerald's depictions in the same genre of the generation to which they also belonged.

Another fine story which takes its flavor from the present but its theme from eternity, is "A Death in the Country."[46] One of Benét's most moving and subtle stories, it enfolds in familiar American images the common tragedy of human experience. Benét weaves in unerringly the sweetness, the formal oppressiveness, the poignancy, ugliness, pretense, and courage that mingle at a small-town funeral. The return of Tom Carroll to Waynesville to attend the rites for his Aunt Louise is simultaneously a return to the darkness of his childhood: for he meets death in the reawakened memory of the mother he lost there when he was a boy, as well as in the present loss of her sister. His wife's recent loss of her mother and her long grief are also fresh in his mind. The triple deaths universalize the theme, though the newest one lends it a sad immediacy.

The changing emotions of Tom and his heightened awareness of the nature of the immortal enemy create the story's meaning, its homely elegy. He had left Waynesville with the memory of his mother and a house, a street, and a family tyrannical through its petty intricacies. He returns as a citizen of New York City, where his existence has taken on the clean contours of modernity. The Waynesville where he had seen his mother's coffin sink into the earth and where the adult relatives had seemed of heroic stature is now scaled down to the trivial dimensions of a trivial way of life. His mother's funeral had been barbarous; Aunt Louise's will be, too.

The turning point in Tom's understanding comes at the church, which he is surprised to find half filled rather than sparsely occupied by old relatives and friends. To his further astonishment, the obsequies are dignified not only by the customary tardy recognition that the living accord the departed, but by the genuine respect and love shown by the mourners. The coffin is ceremonially borne by six Negroes, graduates of the school for freed Negroes which Aunt Louise had made a model institution. The minister's remarks are sincere if banal. And everyone recalls Tom and speaks to him by name, taking his presence for granted. Aunt Louise survives as a presence, an awareness expressed through the general recognition of her individual worth. After the ceremony, Aunt Emmy reveals an unexpected awareness of Tom's worth, of his helpfulness to other members of the family. In a long, salty appraisal of the family, she advises Tom to put down roots, but not in Waynesville. As for death, it must be looked at. The grief will come, but the obsessively fearful flight from death can be halted. Children can be taught not to fear the dark.

"A Death in the Country" suffers drastically in summary because of its complexity and because extracting the meaning strips it of the homely detail of setting and characterization that infuse the story with reality. Through a handful of middle-aged or elderly persons who seem everyone's cousins, Benét brings to life the eternal awkward bond of relatedness—the curious, arbitrarily imposed obligation that transcends friendship yet for the most part lacks warmth and spontaneity. Here are the obnoxious cousin; the forever plump and flustered cousin; the indomitable aunt, calling herself one of those the Fool-Killer will still be looking for on Judgment Day—these and others tightly caught in the irrational and inescapable net of family, yet somehow retaining the essential human ties. In Benét's story they are gathered together by Death in his vulgar American small-town black suit, but not before he makes a respectful bow to the integrity of the individual.

Several other of Benét's stories have death as their central theme, though none of them has the greatness of "A Death in the Country." "Johnny Pye and the Fool-Killer," of course, has its own excellence. A late though inferior story, "The Land Where There Is No Death,"[47] tells of a man's lifelong quest for the realm of permanence, which he finds only in the perception of the necessity of death as a companion to life and an essential of the change without which life would be meaningless. But though death cannot be conquered, neither can life. The story's philosophical content resembles that of "Johnny Pye and the Fool-Killer," but its lack of humor and the highly generalized characterization and setting rob the tale of interest.

According to Rosemary Carr Benét in her introduction to his last collection of short stories, at the time of his death in 1943[48] her husband was working on a piece about the Resurrection. However, his "No Visitors,"[49] published in 1940, following his hospitalization for a nervous breakdown brought on in part by overwork, is a surgically precise exploration of a convalescent writer's state of mind which is cruelly turned into a grimly premonitory state when the doctor recommends a second, even more serious, operation. An expertly constructed story which examines the pathological essence in the experience of hospitalization, it offers no consolation for the mortal lot. This critic, however, would urge an affirmative answer by both Ph.D.'s and common readers to the dying writer's prayer which furnishes the epigraph for the present chapter. If the writer in "No Visitors" was a fictional alter ego of Benét, he was entitled to triple or quadruple the number of his stories which he prayed would find discriminating readers—on and off the campus.

CHAPTER 5

The Propaganda of Freedom

" 'After the last war,' he said, 'the one thing I swore I'd never write was propaganda. But this one is for our skins, and the chips are down.' "

THE WRITER in Benét's short story "The Prodigal Children" believes that by enlisting his talent in World War II he will sacrifice his literary reputation. " 'Remember the fearsome tripe the established names—or most of them—wrote about the last one, and how it retched the bowels of my generation?' " he asks. " 'Well, they'll retch at me just the same way. But somebody had to do it.' "

Benét was one of those who felt he had to do it, and he did it regardless of the cost to his literary reputation, which by 1939 was considerable. Quick to apprehend the nature of the totalitarian menace to democracy during the 1930's, after an initial period of indifference to politics during the first few years of the decade, Benét ended by devoting all his skill and energy to the service of his country. Coming from an Army family, he showed dedication above and beyond the call of duty as a writer of propaganda from the months prior to Pearl Harbor until his death on March 13, 1943.

An official of the Writers War Board classified Benét as one of their "self-starters," meaning that he had already so involved himself in turning out propaganda before the United States entered the war that he needed no assignments from the Board.[1] Benét's activities were too numerous and varied to set forth in this study; his biographer summarizes them in this way:

> Benét's . . . willingness to volunteer his talents for propaganda was limitless and conscientious. The committee chairmen and

their executive secretaries quickly discovered that he would do responsible and thoughtful work for impossible deadlines. He undertook, at the sacrifice of his own work and income and well-being, assignments that were sometimes trivial, sometimes momentous, occasionally inane, always difficult and wearing.[2]

Benét's propaganda writing took him entirely away from his poetry, his short stories, and his novels. However, his justification for this literary digression arose out of the same passionate belief in freedom that generated most of his creative writing. Benét believed that the writer who, like himself, had developed his art under the protection of a democracy had a moral obligation to defend his guardian when it was threatened by tyranny. " 'If the artist believes,' " Benét wrote, " 'I think he should state his belief. It will never be earlier. For neither his freedom of speech nor his liberty of action will automatically preserve themselves.' "[3] Elsewhere he put the choice even more bluntly as being between life and a chance to write, or death and no chance to write.[4]

Benét took issue with Ernest Hemingway when the latter, in his introduction to *Men at War* (1942), asserted that the writer's job is to tell the truth. If conditions made publication of the truth impossible because its revelation would injure his country, Hemingway argued, then the writer should write but voluntarily suppress his work. Benét disagreed.[5] The writer should not, of course, violate his own integrity by writing what he did not believe. If the writer did express his beliefs but wrote badly, the fault was his. Benét himself was untroubled by possible injury to his reputation. At any rate, he could not simply rest on his integrity as a writer "like a hen on a china egg."

The seriousness implicit in Benét's beginning a career quite different from that he had previously chosen did not extend into dogmatic or intolerant attitudes toward writers who did not feel his same sense of duty. He understood that not all writers could turn out propaganda. Longfellow could, but Melville could not.[6] Requesting a propaganda novel from Jane Austen would be foolish, Benét pointed out; and William Blake's reflections on the French Revolution were far removed from reality. Yet the Jane Austens, the Melvilles, and the Blakes are necessary for the survival of literature. Great artists could produce great propaganda, Benét believed, but only when it truly expressed their philosophies.[7] Belief could not be handed to a writer like a benzedrine tablet.

Although Benét voluntarily took command of a battery of propaganda writing assignments, he did not lose sight of the truth that important ideas demand worthy expression. When in 1941 a Conference on Science, Philosophy, and Religion issued a collective statement, Benét criticized its style as " 'the pithless, indeterminate style that disfigures so much of American scholarship. If men are drawing up a new declaration of independence —a declaration of man's spirit, they should do it with at least as much care for the sound and sense and bite of English as Jefferson gave to his own Declaration. . . . [the statement] is pianola-English.' "[8] Important ideas, Benét believed, must be set forth in such a way that they stir the mind.

I   *The Benét Touch*

Whatever the flabbiness of most wartime propaganda, Benét gave to his own versions of it the clarity, naturalness, incisiveness, and native tang that characterized his best literary work. Immersed in American history, keenly aware of the quality of American speech and the contemporary American scene, he brought all his resources to the shaping of words as part of the armament of freedom. His propaganda, whether set forth in the vernacular or in a more philosophical style, has even in retrospect a consistent individuality and distinction. Benét went unerringly to the heart of an issue; and he presented his conclusions in language free of cant, live and lean, and tough with fact and idea. Whether his theme was the certainty of Hitler's defeat or the intellectual atrocities of book-burning, Benét developed his ideas in phrases intelligible to the widest possible domestic audience. He did so without condescension or cheapness, and his propaganda may be read today with respect for both its ideas and its style.

Benét had previously drawn in expert fashion on common speech and folk idiom but he had never adapted either to the special requirements of radio. The degree to which he had become thoroughly professional can be gauged by the ease with which he accommodated himself to his new medium, with its reliance upon music, sound effects, and the human voice. He grasped both the possibilities and limitations of radio, for which he wrote most of his propaganda. Radio was then the best means of reaching a national audience with dramatic effect, and Benét's audience at times numbered many millions. His poetic drama "Listen to the People"[9] which preceded an address by President Roosevelt, was, according to Benét's biographer, heard by more Americans than had ever listened to the words of an important American writer.[10] It had a warm reception in every corner of the nation.

II *Letters to Der Führer*

Benét's most notable script was "Dear Adolf," a series of letters to the Nazi dictator written by representative Americans: a farmer, a worker, a businessman, a housewife, a foreign-born citizen, and a soldier.[11] Benét styles them with speech rhythms, sentence structure, diction, and a point of view which are characteristic enough to make their possessors typical and yet sufficiently individualized to be plausible and interesting. The letter-writers (who were portrayed on the air by such able actors and actresses as Raymond Massey, Melvyn Douglas, James Cagney, and Helen Hayes) fit the needs of propaganda in that they reveal a steadfast determination to do their part to defeat Hitler, but they are not mere idealizations. Benét endows them with humor and something of his own clear-sighted recognition of American weaknesses and limitations, so that the farmer admits that there is never enough rain for him, except when there is too much. When a Negro voice laments the hard lot of his people, the narrator offers no apology but mentions Sojourner Truth and the slow progress of truth. "Dear Adolf" exists today primarily as propaganda rather than art, but it is propaganda of a superior type touched by art, and it should be heard rather than read.

III *An Answer for Daniel Webster*

Benét's finest single radio piece, "We Stand United," followed the bitterly fought national election of 1944.[12] The deep-seated political antagonisms over economic, social, and international issues that were the bitter heritage of the 1930's had been moderated but not buried by the achievements of the New Deal and by the general awareness of national crisis. Benét's direct, moving affirmation of overriding national purpose, and his quiet pride over the ability of the American democracy to conduct a national election while fighting a world war make this script historically significant, and his functional style has a simple dignity appropriate to the occasion. "We Stand United" is Benét's answer to the thunderous query of Daniel Webster, "Neighbor, how stands the Union?" That she stands as she stood, rock-bottomed and copper-sheathed, one and indivisible, was, according to Benét's story, the traditional answer. Benét here, with his eye, as usual, upon the nation's highest destiny, declares that to have argued the issues of the election, to have voted, and to have acted as a people were great achievements, but they were only a beginning. If America's belief in democracy is real, the nation must achieve "the deliberate unity of free men" in the years ahead.

Throughout this short address Benét directs his appeal to the individual, asking him not to submerge his political partisanship but to restrain it short of paralyzing hatred. Obvious though the ideas appear in summary, Benét expresses them so quietly and so trenchantly, and with such an undemanding reliance upon the power and greatness of the American political heritage, that the talk becomes a document worth the study of the serious citizen today. Benét's modest eloquence falters a bit at the end, with a suggested pledge which echoes too many familiar phrases, but when he speaks for himself and sometimes permits himself a bit of poetry, his words register.

IV *America*

Benét was here an American speaking to Americans. In an earlier project undertaken at the request of the Office of War Information, Benét interpreted his country for other nations. His *America*[13] is a short history which was translated into virtually every twentieth-century language.[14] In addition to an Armed Services edition of 121,000 copies, some 50,000 throwaway copies were printed in Italian, German, and other languages, to be left by G.I.'s in whatever country they were liberating.[15] In Hungary *America* was the first book printed after the Nazi hold on the country was broken. What hopes it may have fed in a country gripped by a still stronger tyranny is a matter only of sad speculation. Certainly this book of a hundred-odd pages presents an America which is close to the truth; it is neither the shining republic of super-patriots nor the brutal and corrupt materialism portrayed by radical critics, domestic and foreign. Benét concedes that the nation has not solved every problem and has made mistakes at home and abroad, but he finds its ultimate sanction in the fact that America steadfastly looks to the future of the world and to an international society, secure and free.

In *America* Benét addresses himself to the task of defining the American idea as revealed in our history. Always his focus is upon the building of the heritage of freedom with responsibility. His restricted space limits him to essentials, but he provides brief accounts of the central episodes in the building of the republic and short biographies of some of the more important architects of American freedom, from Franklin down through Lincoln. Along the way he sketches in some of the main traits of the national character, noting, for instance, that even if Americans were handed a complete gold-plated Earthly Paradise they would immediately try to improve it. Not a contemplative people, Americans in the half century after the Civil War neglected thinkers like Willard Gibbs and confined the American Dream to the triune virtues of work, growth, and money. Benét neither condones nor apologizes for the robber-millionaires of this period, but he notes that they did much to build up the economy of the country. The national standard of living rose as a result. In time Theodore Roosevelt denounced the "malefactors of great wealth" and proposed government regulation of the trusts; America did not become a plutocracy. Benét is careful to point out, however, that even in the America of the 1940's, great inequities of wealth and poverty can be found.

In international affairs Benét exhibits equal scrupulousness in evaluating American ethics. He notes that, although the blowing up of the *Maine* was the primary cause of the Spanish-American war, the sinking came after years of strong sentiment for annexation of Cuba. Moreover, American financial interests in Cuba were important, and more American patience and tact could have settled every issue with Spain. However, the American imperialism which ensued—contrary to America's anti-colonial tradition—resulted ultimately in Cuba's becoming a republic, in the Philippines' attaining Commonwealth status, and in Puerto Ricans and Hawaiians being given American citizenship. Benét correctly observes that every imperialistic step the United States has taken has been followed by another step back toward the principles of freedom and independence.

Benét's chronicle concludes with an account of America's twentieth-century abandonment of international isolation. He records President Wilson's Fourteen Points as the culmination of the nation's entry into international politics. The eight principles of the Atlantic Charter are the most recent document setting forth America's international ideals and objectives. Benét's little history concludes by hearkening to voices from the American past, from William Bradford down to Franklin Delano Roosevelt, all of whose words are also America.

The effect of propaganda is impossible to calculate precisely. All that can be tabulated is statistics: copies published and distributed, listeners estimated by research analysts. The consequences of propaganda are still more difficult to estimate. Nevertheless, propaganda can be of major, even of decisive importance in the modern world, as the Nazis and Communists have well understood. Propaganda in the broad sense of the term may well have been of crucial importance in China's movement into the Communist world. Whatever the obstacles in the way of analyzing the effectiveness of propaganda, it is clear that Benét carried out his self-imposed mission with honor and skill. Coming from an Army family, having enlisted in the Army during World War I through the mild deception of memorizing the Army's eye-chart, only to be discharged a few days later for substandard eyesight,[16] Benét in World War II did his utmost for the cause which was blood and bone with him.

Extreme nationalism, as Benét understood, is another form of fanaticism, an extension of individual compulsiveness, arrogance, or extremism, the reflection of a latent or overt tyranny. Benét's conception of propaganda was marked by the tolerance characteristic of his liberalism. His idealism and firm grasp of reality are evident in his wartime writings. Since he quite literally gave them the best of himself, they remain distinguished contributions to the literature of freedom.

CHAPTER 6

Western Star

O powerful western fallen star!
—Whitman[1]

BENÉT'S last fine, though fragmentary, work was published after his death in 1943. *Western Star* was to have been another epic—the *Odyssey* of *American* wandering and seeking—to accompany the *Iliad* that was *John Brown's Body*.[2] Benét had begun taking notes for his second epic as early as 1928, but his responsibilities to his family, which required him to give top priority to his free-lance writing, and his position as American man of letters, which consumed much of his time and energy, drastically curtailed his work upon *Western Star*. In 1941, on the eve of America's entry into the war, Benét, already fully engaged in propaganda work in defense of democracy, put aside the manuscript until peace might enable him to pick it up again.[3]

Like *John Brown's Body*, *Western Star* grew out of Benét's absorption with American history. He conceived of our history as having two major and continuing phases: the preservation of national unity and the restless mobility of our people.[4] "Americans are always moving on," Benét observes in the opening line of the prelude to *Western Star*, and his final plan was to write a poetic history in ten books which would recount the westward push from its beginnings in England to the closing of the areas of free land in America near the end of the nineteenth century.[5] His chief problem he envisioned as that of portraying the changing panorama of frontier life from the perspective of the frontier, rather than from that of the East.[6] His basic method again was to interpret American history through real episodes and both real and imagined characters. Had the other nine books of *Western Star* been equal in length to the single book which Benét completed, the epic would have been three times as long as *John Brown's Body*.

I *Return to Research*

Benét approached his second epic with the same scholarly diligence that had characterized his research into the Civil War, and he was still intent upon breaking through clichés and stereotypes and resurrecting the truth about people and events. In order to master the century and a half of the history which the first book of *Western Star* spanned, he rented a house within driving distance of the Yale University library and immersed himself for months reading histories and original documents. "I have been doing a lot of reading for *Western Star*—Pilgrims, Puritans, Virginians, etc., . . ." he wrote a friend in 1937. "The diaries and letters and such are wonderful—why in hell aren't they better taught in most histories—why don't they let the people come through?"[7]

Besides attempting to rescue people from documentary interment, Benét was actually exploring American history. If anyone had written "even a competent and connected history of the Western frontier from 1745 to 1815," he told the librarian of Yale, "I would feel better. As it is, I continue to take notes in order to form judgments which will probably be wrong when formed. I wish I were writing about Lancelot and Elaine."[8] Frederick Jackson Turner had propounded in 1893 his thesis that the frontier was the dominant force in American history (a thesis which the conception of *Western Star* reflects), but no history of the sort that Benét needed had yet been written. ". . . I wish prominent historians wouldn't contradict each other as much as they do—how's a poor poet to know which is right?"[9] Benét mourned. Actually, at times in *Western Star* Benét is at pains to correct what he regards as historical misconceptions, although the plan of the work as a whole does not involve it heavily in historical controversy.

II *Poet-Historian of Democracy*

As the poet-historian of American democracy, Benét properly centers his narrative upon representative individuals, whether real or fictional, as their lives bear upon or shape in some degree the history of the westering frontier fanning out from England. The agonies of birth and death, the rarer joys and the solace of love, the long hardships of wresting a living from the American wilderness, the ardors and duties of religion—these are Benét's staples. To make them live for the modern American in order to invigorate his love of country and his awareness of the nation's heritage is Benét's aim. He reminds the reader in the short Invocation that

> This was frontier, and this,
> And this, your house, was frontier.

Western Star is thus the testament of nameless multitudes who colonized America and pushed its frontier towards the Pacific. "You shall not win without remembering them," Benét sternly tells the reader in a passage prophetic of the New Frontier of another time of American peril and responsibility for the world's freedom.

III   *The Meaning of the Star*

In the Prelude to *Western Star* Benét, noting the passing of the frontier and with it the "star-rocket" that led the westward surge, poses the question why one should search for any ghostly survival of the star's meaning. He satirizes good-humoredly those foreigners and Americans who have given easy, cut-and-dried answers to the questions of what Americans and Americanism are; and he says that he has no answers beyond the broad ones of the frontier as the shaper of American destiny. And though it is now gone,

> Something remains, obscure to understand,
> But living, and a genius of the land.

And the Prelude ends with the poet hoping to find awakened in himself the wonder felt by the sailors of Columbus on first seeing in the far distance "The line of unimaginable coasts."

Benét here restates the American mysticism that is a major theme of his Invocation for *John Brown's Body*: the essential meaning of America is elusive, too big for definition, though glimpses of it evoke a sense of awe akin to the religious. Benét has seized upon a profound truth about America: that the search for her meaning and destiny must be endless. The quest must return for spiritual nourishment to the monuments, to the history brought to life momentarily, but it must forever pursue the elusive godhead of national soul. A sated America will be a dead America.

In the course of re-creating the American frontier, Benét incidentally makes clear his objections to two old and unfortunately enduring debasements of the American Dream, one corrupt and the other fanatical. After nominating the incredible John Smith of the Pocahontas legend as one of the first Americans, Benét confesses that he likes Smith because he believed till the day of his death that Jamestown had been founded in "a good land." Benét contrasts him with native-born Americans who blessed their country "only while they could milk it dry / And, that being done with, cursed it in the street" (76). He also ticks off prosperous contemporary ladies and gentlemen "Who spent their years despairing of the Republic / And trying ways to beat an income-tax" (76). Although on the whole Benét's portrayal of the Pilgrims presents them very favorably, he refers to their vision as that of "the humble, stupendous arrogance of men / Who are quite sure God is with them" (120). And this first book of the epic concludes with the imminence of "the age of ice" when Puritan zealotry would hang the witches and drive the gentle Quakers from the Zion in the Wilderness.

IV *History Individualized*

In his aim of making American history meaningful through the lives of fictional characters, Benét is more uniformly successful in *Western Star* than in his earlier epic. He is, in fact, consistently successful in the difficult task of contriving men, women, and even children who are of their time, whose lives reflect in one way or another Benét's larger purposes, but who achieve individuality. With the garrulous, vulgar, bawdy, ultimately tragic Mother Billington; with Dickon Heron, the London cocksparrow who ultimately yields to the pull of Devon and the sea; with the pious, awkward Matthew Lanyard; and even with a minor figure like the fading, unscrupulous Sir Gilbert Hay, Benét has dramatized his narrative with interesting and believable people. Like most individuals they are somewhat paradoxical; Henry Shenton, for instance, has "the fearful strength of the gentle." Also, his characters change and develop. The servant-boy Dickon under the heady influence of a free environment resolves to become his own man and does so in Virginia, where he grows tobacco on his own land and is called captain. He and his companions compel our attention when Benét asks us to

listen, now, to the small and human voices,
To the first and stammering voices of the men
Who cling like wasps to the rim of the continent. . . .

(165)

The historical characters are not so numerous as in Benét's first epic, nor, with the exception of John Smith, are they quite so fascinating (a fact that is not Benét's fault), but they are nonetheless incisively recorded. Even though we see them mostly in physically static moments, these figures come alive with a sharp immediacy. We see Sir Walter Raleigh in the Tower of London awaiting his execution, tragically meditating his fate and asking, without hope, of news of Roanoake, where once he was a god; Sir Thomas Smyth, first governor of the East India Company, "the great sage merchant with the golden hand," ruthless, unscrupulous, yet approving the grant of the rights of Englishmen to the colonists at Plymouth; and the swashbuckling John Smith, exulting over the marvelous things he did. These and other portraits are executed surely, precisely, and with just the right amount of detail.

Benét likewise appraises groups like the Pilgrims or even the whole Indian people with insight and judicious perception. Particularly fine is his grasp of the Pilgrims, who, as he points out, were human beings, not merely ancestors (133). In them were both unforced sweetness and iron, and a great practicality. Though they yearned for the bliss of God and groaned at His judgments, they brought along butter, "pease," and beer on the *Mayflower* to avoid scurvy. When a profane sailor was lost, as well as four or five other members of the crew, the Pilgrims knew that God was with them on the sea as on the land, with His great hand outstretched like a cloud.

V *Style and Symbol*

The style of this passage—clear, concrete, near-colloquial, slightly metaphorical—and its loose, easy-moving meter somewhere between blank verse and free verse, with five and six stresses per line, characterize much of *Western Star*. As in *John Brown's Body*, Benét also employs quick-moving, four-stressed couplets of varying length for narration, mostly in the rather jaunty Dickon Heron episodes. The traditional blank verse in the soliloquies is suitably varied, and Benét manages to invest its approximation of speech with the dignities of meditation. The fine Prelude is almost wholly in rhyme, with an irregular, sometimes intricate pattern, and with lines of varying length. Here, as in the rest of the poem, Benét accomodates his verse form to his theme. At times he shifts to ballad meter, which he commands with his usual mastery, especially in "Jack of the Feather's Out Again" (152-56), which recounts a tale of Indian vengeance. A few lyrics sound like small bells amid the masculine and feminine voices of the other meters. Only once does Benét resort to prose for exposition (152), and this passage may have been simply a first-draft note to be transformed into verse when he had the time.

While Benét thus demonstrates the same metrical resourcefulness in *Western Star* that he had evidenced in his first epic, the later work is less varied in style. It is less ambitious and exuberant; Benét no longer daringly tosses the paintbox in his American Pierian Spring to mix a profusion of metaphor and simile that is sometimes brilliant, that sometimes prodigally overspills the narrative. In this respect *Western Star* is more disciplined; it is, as Bernard De Voto observed,[10] the product of a more seasoned narrative poet. On the other hand, Benét still shows his ability to strike off a character in a memorable phrase: the notorious Thomas Morton of Merrymount, foe of the Puritans, "drank the country down like a cup of sack" (166). Benét also devises haunting images such as "lost Iliads of the forest" (70) for the unrecorded wars of the Indians. But this ability is less evident than in *John Brown's Body*, perhaps because the historical figures are not so numerous in *Western Star*. Also, clichés and prosy passages are proportionately more numerous than in the earlier epic. Phrases like "hen's cackle" (28) for an old woman's laugh: "opened their Pandora's box" (51); "it was not a dream" (51); "in childish wonderment" (50); "life . . . stripped to the bone" (113); and "The dice have been cast" (151) are used coins long out of someone else's mint. And such lines as these merely convey information:

> There were a hundred and forty-four, all told,
> In the three small ships. You can read the names, if you like,
> In various spellings. They are English names. . . .

(46)

Another marked difference between the two epics lies in imagery and symbol. The star is the equivalent of John Brown as a unifying device, but of course it does not have any historical or myth-making function. It appears only in the Prelude and at the end of this first book of the poem, gleaming over the endless forests of the West as Dickon's sons prepare to follow it, the lure and ideal, unattainable, undefinable. Yet neither the star nor any other symbol has anything like the manifold functions of John Brown or the Phaeton clock. For this and other reasons, *Western Star* is less dense in meaning than the earlier epic.

Criticism of *Western Star* must be qualified by the consideration that it is a fragment which Benét doubtless would have polished had he lived. He intended his second epic to be his finest poem; and, in 1939, during one of his last extended periods of work on it, a friend noted that he was constantly revising it.[11] Benét's brief apologia near the end of the first part of his projected epic should also be heeded:

> If this song is
> Crooked as rivers, rough as the mountain-range
> And many-tongued and a wanderer to the end,
> It must be so, for it follows the giant land,
> It follows the ways and the roads and the wanderings,
> Not one man's fate.

(164)

Western Star was a casualty of World War II in almost the same sense that its author was. Had Stephen Vincent Benét lived to follow his star to its zenith above the vanished frontier, it might have shone as a star of high magnitude. Even above today's New Frontier it forms, with its twin, an axis for a constellation unique in the broad skies of American literature.

CHAPTER 7

In Retrospect

BENÉT'S CAREER is notable for its tragic brevity, its frustrations, its diversity, and its relative richness and productivity. Despite the handicap of ill health, Benét did not allow his physical torments to lessen appreciably the quantity of his work or to affect its form or content. During thirteen of his most creative years, from 1930 until his death in 1943 at the age of forty-four, he was seldom blessed with normal good health; he was often tortured by arthritis of the spine and other ailments.[1] During his last four or five years his many self-imposed duties as a wartime writer repeatedly drained him of his reserves of energy, but he somehow replenished them from deep spiritual and physical resources, until the latter failed him. His courage, his sense of humor, and his talents did not fail him.

Although Benét's decision to write propaganda for democracy sharply curtailed his purely literary output, the wisdom of his choice is hardly to be questioned. His radio dramas and *America* were the products of a moral imperative for Benét—one as categorical for him as Kant's are for mankind. The preservation and extension of freedom with responsibility had for Benét an absolute sanction which in peacetime blessed the conceptions of his best poetry and fiction. It is irrelevant to argue that completion of another epic, even if it turned out to be his finest work, would be a greater contribution to democracy—literary fare that would nourish American audiences yet unborn—than anything he could write for immediate purposes. Benét simply could not devote himself to "art" when tyranny had placed in hideous jeopardy the freedom that he regarded as the necessary condition for all significant expressions of the human mind and spirit.

I *The Free-Lance Gamble*

Nor can much objection be legitimately raised against Benét's yielding to the other necessity which choked off an indeterminate amount of his free creativity. Throughout his adult life Benét made his way in one of the toughest, most financially hazardous professions. Time and again his bank account was down to a few dollars. His responsibilities were doubled when he married, and then they multiplied successively when his three children were born. A fine husband and father, he wanted his family to live in pleasant, comfortable circumstances; moreover, he had his own tastes for gracious living to satisfy. The academic life which might have offered a solution for a writer who wanted freedom to write what he pleased he rejected, partly because of its low salaries, partly because of its social restrictions.[2] The good life for him was neither austere nor secluded but active, various, and physically, emotionally, and socially rich.

The primary effect of Benét's free-lance career upon his writings was, of course, to cheapen many of them for sale to the mass-circulation magazines that would pay him the most. His short stories, which became his bread-and-butter product, were most drastically affected by his financial exigencies; of the hundred and fifty which were published, approximately two thirds are valueless because they were written for an audience with fixed, narrow tastes—or so editors regarded them. It is intriguing to speculate about what Benét might have written had he been granted some sort of super-Guggenheim fellowship that would have given him the freedom from deadlines and bills he needed but had enjoyed only once in his career. It was the Guggenheim Foundation that enabled him to write *John Brown's Body*. His extended eighteen-month fellowship provided him, he said, "the leisure to write the sort of thing I felt was worth while, and I did so, not thinking of results."[3] He was never again to have such an opportunity. The fame and financial security he eventually attained doubtless would have given him more chances after World War II, but fate was not to permit them.

Benét's free-lance career cost him in other ways. Writing short stories went against his grain, and he was constantly uneasy with or rebellious against the demands of editors for formula fiction. His critical sense was always keen; it was hyper-keen when he turned it on his own work, which he frequently underrated. At times his writer's conscience revolted, notably when he refused to sugar the plot of his novel *Spanish Bayonet* to suit editorial and public tastes for happy endings. In this instance his sense of honor overcame even his strong love for his family: the sacrifice of the ten thousand dollars offered him for serial rights caused genuine economic distress for his wife and children as well as for himself.[4] His early stories about the American past, which include some of his best, were turned down by the editors of all magazines except those of *Country Gentleman* and the *Elks' Magazine*.[5] The subsequent popularity and widespread acceptance of such tales came in spite of editorial stuffiness, and they represent a triumph of Benét's determination and imagination. More often, however, his fiction was constricted by economic pressure.

Despite the mutilations and adulteration that Benét's decisions about his career inflicted on his literary product, the consequences were not all bad. The risks of free-lancing appealed to the gambler's instinct in Benét; his essential courage made him prefer uncertainty and excitement to safety. "Life's too brief and insecure," he said, "not to play everything you have on the appearance of Little Joe, even when you have no logical reason to suppose he will emerge."[6] He felt that a more worth-while life was gained by "alternating feasts and semistarvation than by a continual safe existence in Childs restaurants."[7] And although his hack work often crowded out serious writing, particularly poetry, the marketability of short stories eventually led Benét into writing a group of memorable ones.

II *New Directions*

He never wholly freed himself from commercial considerations, and even some of his better stories are marred by an occasional statement of the obvious. Yet he was never content to be merely a producer of profitable fiction and poetry or to capitalize on any of the other easy techniques for marketing his talents, such as lecturing or advising at writers' conferences. His steadily growing reputation during the 1930's, much of it permanently assured by *John Brown's Body*, would have made it easy for Benét to capitalize on his fame by facile repetitions of his successes.[3] He was aware of this danger when he observed: "It is one of the hardest things in the world for the popular writer who has made a success at one sort of thing to branch out into another field. The bread-and-butter pressure is all the other way. 'Give us some more of your delightful stories about Southern mountaineers—or New York policemen—or Andaman islanders.' "[9]

Benét chose to pioneer. His creative drive, his independence, and his growing fear of the totalitarian threat to democracy led him to strike out in new directions in his prose and poetry. Only one of his prophetic poems was first-rate, but as a group they were superior to the similar poems of any of his contemporaries except for Carl Sandburg's *The People, Yes.* "The Devil and Daniel Webster," "Johnny Pye and the Fool-Killer," "The Last of the Legions," and "The Place of the Gods" were among the distinguished stories that Benét wrote during the late 1930's. When he turned to the new field of radio drama as the best medium for his contribution to the defense of freedom, he produced the rarest sort of propaganda—that which has significance and literary merit decades after the war which occasioned it.

III *Benét's Versatility and Appeal*

Benét's extraordinary ability to master one genre after another makes him one of the most versatile of American writers. His scope goes beyond what has previously been indicated in this study. His radio drama "A Child Is Born,"[10] for example, which was originally produced with Alfred Lunt and Lynn Fontanne in the leading roles, is an effective treatment of one of the most difficult of themes, the nativity of Christ. Benét had had a deep interest in the theatre since his days at Yale, and in the early 1920's he collaborated in the writing of two plays which were produced in New York.[11] They closed almost immediately, but in 1937 Benét and Douglas Moore, a composer interested in American folk material, made of Washington Irving's "The Legend of Sleepy Hollow" a short operetta which was nationally broadcast by the National Broadcasting Company and was later published for professional use.[12] In 1938 the two turned "The Devil and Daniel Webster" into an opera which was produced by the American Lyric Theatre in New York. It was enthusiastically received by audiences and critics; Brooks Atkinson, for example, praised it in the *New York Times* as representing "some of the finest and most painstaking work of the season."[13]

Benét's best work in all fields possesses this magic quality of appealing to both the mass audience and those intellectuals who do not assume that every piece of literature which enjoys national popularity is *ipso facto* superficial. It is sometimes forgotten that great literary and dramatic works have profoundly moved both simple and sophisticated audiences. Shakespeare's plays are the most obvious example. Benét's stature as a writer was modest, but in his finest work artistry and meaning fuse to satisfy discriminating veteran tastes as well as those of less experienced readers.

Benét has such a broad attraction for Americans because he skillfully and lovingly drew upon the American heritage of freedom and because he understood past and present challenges to that freedom. His mind was infused with the spirit of the tolerant, undogmatic, humanitarian, hard-headedly optimistic liberalism that has moved the nation in the most crucial phases of its history and has characterized its greatest leaders from Jefferson to Kennedy. Benét's patriotism sometimes expressed itself in implicit pride in America and her great and common men; sometimes it celebrated America's lyric beauty or noted her salty individuality; sometimes it rollicked with folk laughter or scorned complacency or arrogant wealth; more often it gravely warned of the dangers to the Union. Benét's love of his country was strong and manly, but it could be as tender as his love for his wife. Never did his voice rise to stridency or bravado; no fair-minded foreigner can take offense at a single line. The Daniel Webster tales ride on a superb humor that outraces national pride at the point where it might become chauvinism; patriotism in Benét is so civilized that it tends to advance world civilization.

IV *The National Writer*

Benét was a twentieth-century product of strong currents in American literature as well as in American history. He was a national writer of the sort that Emerson and Whitman had been and that many minor figures had attempted to be or had called for; as a poet he shares this honor with Carl Sandburg. The demand for American writers at the birth of the Republic was fundamentally a demand for a literature worthy of the new nation. It was not until Emerson's address "The American Scholar" in 1837 that there was clear recognition of the need for a literature, indeed, a whole culture, free and independent of Europe, though willing to make use of its best thought and art. As far back as the late eighteenth century, Joel Barlow had written an American epic, and in one form or another a vague notion of a great literary work commensurate with the greatness of America persisted through the nineteenth and into the twentieth century. Treating the original classical form in a free and independent manner, *John Brown's Body* and *Western Star* and Sandburg's *The People, Yes* are the finest modern expressions of this aim.

The fact that Benét's romanticism originally derived from William Morris had unfortunate consequences, for it influenced him to rework banal themes and imagery and encouraged a thin and overly emotional treatment of material. It led him into a surface richness, a lyric fluency, and perhaps a flexibility of narrative form; but the boldness and optimism of American romanticism and certain of its historical and political perspectives were in the long run much more valuable to him. They were not, however, any more essential to him than the realism which informs his scrupulous historical studies, his unsparing scrutiny of the contemporary world, and his late-maturing political views. The folk humor and idiom which characterize such stories as "Johnny Pye and the Fool-Killer" and the Daniel Webster tales, woven of footloose fantasy, poetry, and homely realism, have their antecedents in the yarn spinners of the Old Southwest and in Mark Twain.[14] Benét's style in his mature work is modern in that it lies closer to the rhythms and vocabulary of ordinary speech than to the elevated, decorous, and rhetorical style that died a lingering death in the nineteenth century. The style of Benét's poetry is generally modern, but his forms have some allegiance to tradition.

Benét's mind was quick, sensitive, flexible, acute, constantly reacting to its surroundings but moving easily into the past, usually as the critical point of reference for the present or future. Benét's ancestry was Minorcan, or Spanish, but his intellect had the French quality of clarity, and his sensibility was often gay and vivacious in the French manner. His intellect was keen rather than profound; its affinity was for history and art and people rather than for philosophy or religion. Its litheness was one of its strong points, but this trait could slide into superficiality or sensationalism. However, the ambiguous treatment of religion in his writings, with Christianity sometimes scoffed at in the mood of irreverence or skepticism of the 1920's yet more often treated with high seriousness if not faith, gives way to a religious attitude toward American destiny.

Benét's intellectual range was roughly commensurate with the scope of his sensibility; his emotional spectrum runs from the darkest national tragedy to the sunniest morning humor. A dismal quirk, a grim, distorted, ironic, even terrible vision of life occasionally appears in a poem, a story, or an episode in a novel, but Benét's courage, humanism, and good sense normally moved him to a temperate affirmation or at least to the positive action of warning. A dozen or more fine short stories, a thoughtful novel, a handful of lyrics about love and America, some memorable documents in the long history of freedom, an impressive epic and an epic fragment—these are Benét's gifts to the land he cherished. They deserve to be read by the Americans whom they may teach and delight.

Notes and References

Preface

1. Benét, "Annotated Edition," *Atlantic Monthly*, CLXXII(October, 1943), 55. Reprinted in *The Last Circle* (New York, 1946), pp. 3-4.

2. Laura Bergquist, "Jacqueline: What You Don't Know about Our First Lady," *Look*, XXV (July 4, 1961), 61-62.

Chapter One

1. Charles A. Fenton, *Stephen Vincent Benét: The Life and Times of an American Man of Letters, 1898-1943* (New Haven, Conn., 1958), pp. 36, 41, 96, and *passim*. Hereafter in these footnotes this work will be referred to as *Benét*.

2. *John Brown's Body* (Garden City, N.Y., 1928). This work has gone through a number of editions. The twenty-first, edited by Mabel A. Bessey (New York, 1941) is the one cited in the present study.

3. Introduction to *Stephen Vincent Benét: Selected Poetry and Prose* (New York, 1960).

4. Benét, letter to Paul Engle, Oct. 4, 1935, *Selected Letters of Stephen Vincent Benét*, ed. Charles A. Fenton (New Haven, Conn., 1960), p. 279. Hereafter this collection will be referred to as *Letters*.

5. Fenton, *Benét*, p. 41.

6. Privately printed by the Brick Row Book Shop, New Haven, Conn., 1917; reprinted in Benét's later collection of poetry, *Young Adventure* (Yale University Press, 1918).

7. Fenton, *Benét*, p. 56.

8. "The Hemp" appeared originally in *Century Magazine*, XCI (January, 1916), 342. Reprinted in *Selected Works of Stephen Vincent Benét*, 2 vols., ed. unidentified (New York, 1942), I, 371-75.

9. "Three Days' Ride," according to Fenton (*Benét*, n. 383), appeared originally in the *Yale Literary Magazine*, LXXXI (1915-16), 13. Reprinted in *Selected Works*, I, 389-92.

10. *Heavens and Earth*, pp. 30-37.

11. "The Mountain Whippoorwill" appeared first in *Century Magazine*, XXCVII (March, 1925), 635-39. Reprinted in *Tiger Joy, Ballads and Poems*, and *Selected Works*, I, 376-80.

12. "King David" was first published in the *Nation,* CXVI (Feb. 14, 1923), 117-79. Also published separately under the same title by Henry Holt & Co. in 1923; was included in *Tiger Joy, Ballads and Poems,* and *Selected Works,* I, 368-70.

13. "The Ballad of William Sycamore, 1790-1880" first appeared in the *New Republic,* XXXII (Nov. 8, 1922), 279. It was republished by the *Literary Digest,* LXXV (Nov. 25, 1922), 36, and by the Brick Row Book Shop, New York, 1923, as *The Ballad of William Sycamore.* Reprinted, *Tiger Joy, Ballads and Poems,* and *Selected Works,* I, 368-70. Benét changed the *New Republic* subtitle to "1790-1871" in subsequent printings. See Fenton, *Benét,* n. 9, p. 390.

14. Fenton, *Benét,* p. 148.

15. *Ibid.*

16. In *The Literary History of the United States,* 3 vols., eds. Spiller, Thorp, Johnson, and Canby (New York, 1946), II, 1350-51. See Fenton, *Benét,* pp. 126-29 for an analysis of the critical reception of the poem.

17. "American Names," *Yale Review,* XVII (Oct., 1927), 63-64. Reprinted, *Ballads and Poems,* pp. 3-4, and *Selected Works,* I, 367-68.

18. Fenton, *Benét,* p. 190.

19. See *Life,* XVI, 5 (Jan., 1931), 48-56, for a photographic essay on the American place-names in the poem.

20. "Wounded Knee," *Dictionary of American History* (New York, 1940), ed. James Truslow Adams.

21. *Selected Works,* I, 408.

22. Letter to Rosemary Carr, April 21, 1921, in *Letters,* p. 55.

23. *Selected Works,* I, 363-64.

24. Reprinted in *Selected Works,* I, 339-41.

25. *Ibid.,* pp. 343-44.

26. *Ibid.,* pp. 342-43.

27. *Burning City,* (New York, 1936) p. 53; *Selected Works,* I, 364.

28. See Fenton, *Benét, passim.*

29. *Selected Works,* I, 362.

30. *The Last Circle* (New York, 1946), pp. 303-4.

31. Fenton, *Benét,* pp. 255-56.

32. *Selected Works,* I, 409.

33. *Ibid.,* pp. 411-12.

34. *New Yorker,* XIV (Apr. 12, 1938), 21; *Selected Works,* I, 461-63.

35. "The American Grain," *Poetry,* XLVIII (August, 1936), 276-82.

36. *New Yorker,* XIV (Apr. 12, 1938). Reprinted in *Selected Works,* I, 457-61.

37. *Selected Works,* I, 464-68. "Nightmare at Noon" originally appeared in the *New York Times.*

Chapter Two

1. *John Brown's Body,* ed. Mabel A. Bessey (21st ed.; New York, 1941).
2. Fenton, *Benét,* pp. 185-88.
3. *Ibid.,* p. 189.
4. *Ibid.,* p. 181.
5. "The Phaeton Symbol in *John Brown's Body,*" *American Literature,* XVIII (November, 1945), 231-42.
6. Ovid, *The Metamorphoses,* trans. Horace Gregory (New York, 1958).
7. *Ibid.,* p. 66.
8. Fenton, *Benét,* p. 182.
9. *Ibid.*
10. "The Irrepressible Conflict," *Nation,* CXXVII (Sept. 19, 1928), 274.
11. Fenton, *Benét,* p. 218.
12. "Introduction," *Stephen Vincent Benét; Selected Poetry and Prose,* p. xi.
13. See Christopher La Farge's "The Narrative Poetry of Stephen Vincent Benét," *Saturday Review of Literature,* XXVII (Aug. 5, 1944), 106-8, for a discerning analysis of Benét's technical achievements.
14. "The Irrepressible Conflict."
15. *The Literary History of the United States,* II, 1350.

Chapter Three

1. Fenton, *Benét,* pp. 94-95.
2. See Fenton, *Benét,* pp. 108-18 *passim* for an account of the writing of the novel.
3. Fenton, *Benét,* pp. 112-13.
4. *Ibid.,* p. 114.
5. *Ibid.,* p. 116.
6. *Ibid.,* p. 106.
7. *Ibid.,* p. 105.
8. See Fenton, *Benét,* pp. 155-63 *passim* for an account of the writing of the novel, including Benét's problems with a magazine publisher.
9. Fenton, *Benét,* p. 142.
10. *Ibid.,* p. 156.
11. *Ibid.,* p. 268.
12. *Ibid.,* p. 269.
13. *Ibid.,* p. 266.
14. *Ibid.,* p. 272.

Chapter Four

1. Fenton, *Benét*, p. 123.
2. *Ibid.*, p. 339.
3. *Ibid.*, p. 123.
4. Benét, "O'Brien's Choice" (review of *Fifty Best American Short Stories, 1914-1939*, ed. Edward J. O'Brien), *Saturday Review of Literature*, XX (July 8, 1939), 5.
5. Fenton, *Benét*, p. 177.
6. *Ibid.*
7. *Ibid.*, p. 285.
8. *Ibid.*, p. 169.
9. *Saturday Evening Post*, CCIX (Oct. 24, 1936), 8-9, 68-74. Reprinted in *Thirteen O'Clock* (New York, 1937) and *Selected Works*, II, 32-46.
10. *Saturday Evening Post*, CCIX (May 22, 1937), 18-19, 100-5. Reprinted in *Thirteen O'Clock*.
11. *Saturday Evening Post*, CCXII (Oct. 28, 1939), 18-19, 40-47.
12. *Saturday Evening Post*, CCX (May 14, 1938), 12-13, 74-78. Reprinted in *Tales Before Midnight* (New York, 1939) and *Selected Works*, II, 3-16.
13. *Atlantic Monthly*, CLX (December, 1937), 681-90. Reprinted in *Selected Works*, II, 17-31.
14. *Saturday Evening Post*, CCXII (May 18, 1940), 12-13, 86-92. Reprinted in *Selected Works*, II, 46-59.
15. *Saturday Evening Post*, CCX (Sept. 18, 1937), 10-11, 37-44. Reprinted in *Selected Works*, II, 90-100, and as a separate work, *Johnny Pye and the Fool-Killer* (Weston, Vt., 1938).
16. *Country Gentleman*, XCI (May, 1926), 6-7, 74-79. Reprinted in *Thirteen O'Clock*.
17. Fenton, *Benét*, pp. 292, 294.
18. *Ibid.*, p. 293.
19. *Ibid.*, p. 127.
20. *Ibid.*, p. 295.
21. *Ibid.* The source of Benét's remark is Robert Van Gelder's "Mr. Benét's Work in Progress," *New York Times Book Review*, VI (April 21, 1940), 20.
22. *McCall's*, LXVIII (October, 1940), 14-15, 89-94. Reprinted in *The Last Circle*.
23. *Selected Works*, II, 46-59.
24. Fenton, *Benét*, p. 365.
25. *Selected Works*, II, 90-100.
26. *Atlantic Monthly*, CLXVIII (November, 1941), 539-48. Reprinted in *The Last Circle*.

27. *Country Gentleman,* CVIII (May, 1938), 10-11, 72-74. Reprinted in *Tales Before Midnight* and *Selected Works,* II, 59-74.

28. *Saturday Evening Post,* CCIX (Sept. 5, 1936), 8-9, 34-38. Reprinted in *Thirteen O'Clock* and *Selected Works,* II, 412-30.

29. *Atlantic Monthly,* CLXX (August, 1942), 41-48. Reprinted in *The Last Circle.*

30. Fenton, *Benét,* p. 365.

31. *Harper's Bazaar* (February, 1929), 192-99. Reprinted in *Thirteen O'Clock* and *Selected Works,* II, 398-412.

32. This story was originally titled "The Place of the Gods," *Saturday Evening Post,* CCX (July 31, 1937), 10-11, 59-60. Reprinted in *Thirteen O'Clock* and *Selected Works,* II, 471-83.

33. Fenton, *Benét,* p. 335.

34. *Saturday Evening Post,* CCXV (Feb. 6, 1943), 14-15, 49-53. Reprinted in *The Last Circle.*

35. *Saturday Evening Post,* CCX (Nov. 6, 1937), 18-19, 81-85. Reprinted in *Tales Before Midnight* and *Selected Works,* II, 430-44.

36. *Ladies' Home Journal,* LVI (May, 1939), 16-17, 41-43. Reprinted in *Tales Before Midnight* and *Selected Works,* II, 461-71.

37. Fenton, *Benét,* p. 338.

38. *Saturday Evening Post,* CCIX (Dec. 12, 1936), 5-6, 100-5. Reprinted in *Thirteen O'Clock* and *Selected Works,* II, 444-60.

39. *Saturday Evening Post,* CCVIII (Oct. 5, 1935), 16-17, 78-81. Reprinted in *Thirteen O'Clock* and *Selected Works,* II, 383-98.

40. *Saturday Evening Post,* CCXIV (Feb. 14, 1942), 9-11, 76-80. Reprinted in *The Last Circle.*

41. This story was originally published as "Schooner's Class," *Collier's,* CI (June 18, 1938), 14-15, 65-67. Reprinted in *Tales Before Midnight* and *Selected Works,* II, 286-300.

42. *Saturday Evening Post,* CCIX (Sept. 5, 1936), 8-9, 34-38. Reprinted in *Thirteen O'Clock* and *Selected Works,* II, 301-18.

43. *Century Magazine,* CXVI (October, 1928), 751-59. Reprinted in *Selected Works,* II, 273-86.

44. *Delineator,* CXXII (June, 1933), 13-14, 40-41. Reprinted in *Selected Works,* II, 261-73.

45. *Saturday Evening Post,* CCXV (Dec. 19, 1942), 16-17, 80-83. Reprinted in *The Last Circle.*

46. *Harper's Magazine,* CLXIV (March 1, 1932), 427-40. Reprinted in *Thirteen O'Clock* and *Selected Works,* II, 359-79.

47. *Redbook,* LXXIX (October, 1942), 40-43, 65-69. Reprinted in *The Last Circle.*

48. *The Last Circle,* p. vii.

49. *Saturday Evening Post,* CCXII (March 16, 1940), 12-13, 59-62. Reprinted in *Selected Works,* II, 346-59.

Chapter Five

1. Letter from Mrs. Alvan L. Barach to Charles A. Fenton, June 13, 1957; cited in Fenton, *Benét*, p. 355.
2. *Ibid.*, p. 358.
3. *Ibid.*, p. 357.
4. *Ibid.*
5. *Ibid.*
6. *Ibid.*, p. 355.
7. *Ibid.*, pp. 357-58.
8. *Ibid.*, p. 358.
9. *We Stand United, and Other Radio Scripts* (New York, 1945), 135-54.
10. Fenton, *Benét*, pp. 364-65.
11. *We Stand United*, pp. 9-67.
12. *Ibid.*, pp. 3-8.
13. *America* (New York, 1944).
14. Fenton, *Benét*, p. 372.
15. Letter from Jean Crawford of Holt, Rinehart and Winston, Inc., to P. E. S., Oct. 9, 1961.
16. Fenton, *Benét*, p. 73.

Chapter Six

1. Henry Seidel Canby noted the spiritual link between Whitman and Benét as indicated by the resemblance between the title of Benét's work and the line from Whitman's Lincoln elegy, "When Lilacs Last in the Dooryard Bloom'd." "As We Remember Him," symposium by fourteen contemporaries, *Saturday Review of Literature*, XXVI (March 27, 1943), 7-11.
2. Fenton, *Benét*, p. 344.
3. *Ibid.*, p. 353.
4. *Ibid.*, p. 344.
5. *Ibid.*, p. 345.
6. *Ibid.*, pp. 345-46.
7. Letter to Paul Engle, Sept. 16, 1937, *Letters*, pp. 302-3.
8. Letter to Bernhard Knollenberg, Dec. 24, 1940, *Letters*, pp. 359-60.
9. Letter to Carl Brandt, Aug. 11, 1938, *Letters*, p. 313.
10. Review of *Western Star*, *New York Times Book Review*, Sec. 7 (June 27, 1943), 1.
11. Fenton, *Benét*, p. 350.

Chapter Seven

1. Fenton, "Introduction," *Letters,* p. xxiv.
2. Fenton, *Benét,* pp. 89-91 *passim.*
3. *Ibid.,* p. 194.
4. *Ibid.,* p. 164.
5. *Ibid.,* p. 275.
6. *Ibid.,* p. 146.
7. *Ibid.*
8. *Ibid.,* pp. 274-76.
9. Benét and Rosemary Carr Benét, "Mary Roberts Rinehart's Bread and Butter," *New York Herald Tribune Books,* IX (Oct. 19, 1947), 7.
10. *We Stand United,* pp. 155-81.
11. Fenton, *Benét,* pp. 135-41.
12. *Ibid.,* p. 351.
13. "Cheating the Devil to Music," *New York Times* (May 21, 1939), p. 1.
14. Walter Blair, "Stephen Vincent Benét," *The Literature of the United States,* eds. Blair, Hornberger, and Stewart (Chicago, 1953), II, 1005-6.

Selected Bibliography

PRIMARY SOURCES

America. New York: Farrar and Rinehart, Inc., 1944.
Ballads and Poems, 1915-1930. Garden City, N.Y.: Doubleday, Doran and Co., Inc., 1931.
Ballad of the Duke's Mercy. New York: House of Books, 1939.
The Ballad of William Sycamore. New York: Brick Row Book Shop, 1923.
The Beginning of Wisdom. New York: Henry Holt and Co., 1921.
A Book of Americans. (Written in collaboration with Rosemary Carr Benét.) New York: Farrar and Rinehart, Inc., 1933.
Burning City. New York: Farrar and Rinehart, Inc., 1936.
A Child Is Born: A Modern Drama of the Nativity. Boston: W. H. Baker, 1942.
Dear Adolf. New York: Farrar and Rinehart, Inc., 1942.
The Devil and Daniel Webster. Weston, Vt.: Countryman Press, 1937.
The Devil and Daniel Webster. (One-act play.) New York: Dramatists Play Service, 1939. (The motion picture version, *All That Money Can Buy*, has been collected in John Gassner's *Twenty Best Film Plays*, New York: Crown Publishers, 1943.)
The Devil and Daniel Webster. (Libretto.) New York: Farrar and Rinehart, Inc., 1939.
The Drug Shop; or, Endymion in Edmonstown. (Privately printed.) New Haven, Connecticut: Brick Row Book Shop, 1917.
Five Men and Pompey: a Series of Dramatic Portraits. Boston: Four Seas Co., 1915.
The Headless Horseman. (Libretto.) Boston: Schirmer Co., 1927.
Heavens and Earth. New York: Henry Holt and Co., 1920.
James Shore's Daughter. Garden City, N.Y.: Doubleday, Doran and Co., Inc., 1934.
Jean Huguenot. New York: Henry Holt and Co., 1923.
John Brown's Body. Garden City, N.Y.: Doubleday, Doran and Co., 1928.
John Brown's Body. Twenty-first edition, edited and annotated by Mabel A. Bessey, with an introductory essay, "The Coming of the American Civil War," by Bert James Loewenberg. New York: Rinehart and Co., Inc., 1941.
Johnny Pye and the Fool-Killer. Weston, Vt.: Countryman Press, 1938.
King David. New York: Farrar, Strauss and Co., 1946.

The Last Circle. New York: Farrar, Strauss and Co., 1946.
Listen to the People. New York: Council for Democracy, 1941.
Nightmare at Noon. New York: Farrar and Rinehart, Inc., 1940.
Selected Works of Stephen Vincent Benét. 2 vols. Introduction by
    Basil Davenport. (Name of editor is not given.) New York:
    Rinehart and Co., Inc., 1942.
Spanish Bayonet. New York: George H. Doran Co., 1926.
Stephen Vincent Benét, Selected Poetry and Prose. Edited with an
    introduction by Basil Davenport. New York: Rinehart and Co.,
    Inc., 1942. (This paperback edition is considerably less extensive
    than the hardback edition listed above but contains a few poems
    and short stories not in the other selection.)
Tales Before Midnight. New York: Farrar and Rinehart, Inc., 1939.
Thirteen O'Clock. New York: Farrar and Rinehart, Inc., 1937.
Tiger Joy. New York: George H. Doran Co., 1925.
Twenty-Five Short Stories. Garden City, N.Y.: Sun Dial Press, 1943.
We Stand United, and Other Radio Scripts. New York: Farrar and
    Rinehart, Inc., 1945.
Western Star. New York: Farrar and Rinehart, Inc., 1943.
Young Adventure. New Haven, Conn.: Yale University Press, 1918.
Young People's Pride. New York: Henry Holt and Co., 1922.

SECONDARY SOURCES

I. *Criticism and Biography*

Criticism of Benét's writings is scanty. Aside from Charles A.
Fenton's critical biography, no full-length study has appeared, and
significant essays are few. Reviews of individual works, of course,
become increasingly numerous during Benét's rising and expanding
career, but to include an adequate list of these in this bibliography is
not feasible. I have, instead, cited a few of the more important
reviews, chosen rather arbitrarily.

ALLDREDGE, CHARLES. Review of *Western Star, Nation,* CLVII (July
    31, 1943), 132. Rightly observes that much modern poetry has
    digressed too far from the central concerns of life; capably
    defends Benét as one of the few contemporary poets able to
    write relatively popular and significant poetry which is not
    meretricious.
"As We Remember Him." A symposium by fourteen contemporaries
    who knew Benét. *Saturday Review of Literature,* XXVI (March
    27, 1943), 7-11. Leonard Bacon, Phillip Barry, William Rose
    Benét, John Berdan, Henry Seidel Canby, Carl Carmer, John
    Farrar, Jeremy Ingalls, Christopher La Farge, Archibald

MacLeish, Christopher Morley, William Lyon Phelps, Muriel Rukeyser, and Thornton Wilder in brief memorials compile a valuable biographical piece. Some of the tributes, especially Canby's, have critical importance as well.

DAVENPORT, BASIL. "Introduction," *Stephen Vincent Benét, Selected Poetry and Prose.* New York: Rinehart and Co., Inc., 1960. A short biographical, critical, and historical essay; sound and suitable for the reader unacquainted with Benét and his work.

ENGLE, PAUL. "The American Search." Review of *Western Star. Poetry,* LXIII (December, 1943), 159-62. Sensibly takes a middle ground between modernists and traditionalists in poetry and places Benét in it.

FENTON, CHARLES A., ed. *Selected Letters of Stephen Vincent Benét.* New Haven, Conn.: Yale University Press, 1960. A highly readable selection of Benét's short, incisive, distinctive letters which throws much light on his mind and career and on the literary scene during the 1920's, 1930's, and early 1940's.

————. *Stephen Vincent Benét: The Life and Times of an American Man of Letters, 1898-1943.* New Haven, Conn.: Yale University Press, 1958. An excellent critical biography, thorough, well-proportioned, judicious. Fenton admires Benét, with good reason, but is not dazzled by him; and his critical judgments, though necessarily limited in scope, are nearly always sound and frequently show keen insight. This biography is unlikely to be superseded.

KREYMBORG, ALFRED. *Our Singing Strength: A History of American Poetry.* New York: Tudor Publishing Co., 1929, pp. 607-11. Primarily concerned with *John Brown's Body.* A discriminating evaluation praising Benét's poetic achievements, humanitarian philosophy, and epic purpose; limited, however, by a conventional formalistic approach.

LA FARGE, CHRISTOPHER. "The Narrative Poetry of Stephen Vincent Benét," *Saturday Review of Literature,* XXVII (Aug. 5, 1944), 106-8. Partially disqualifying himself as critic because of friendship for Benét and lack of historical perspective, La Farge nevertheless succeeds in analyzing clearly Benét's achievements.

MATTHIESSEN, F. O. "The New Poetry," *The Literary History of the United States,* II (New York: Macmillan, 1946), 1350-51. Brief appraisal of major importance because of the eminence of this critic and scholar and of the history. Largely factual, but correctly points out that *John Brown's Body* raises the problem of popular art in a democracy. Errs, however, in implying that Harriet Monroe's review of the epic (see below) is derogatory. Matthiessen and Zabel (see below) have probably been responsible for lowering Benét's reputation in academic circles.

MONROE, HARRIET. "A Cinema Epic," *Poetry,* XXXIII (1928), 91-96.

A slightly equivocal review, although the apparently deprecatory title is not borne out by the prevailing enthusiasm for *John Brown's Body* on the part of the founder of *Poetry*. An interesting, generally valid interpretation.

TATE, ALLEN. "The Irrepressible Conflict," *Nation*, CXXVII (Sept. 19, 1928), 274. Denies that *John Brown's Body* is an epic; erroneously charges Benét with the lack of a central conception, but perceives the scope of the work and points out a number of Benét's achievements. A balance of favorable and unfavorable judgments, tentatively tipped slightly toward favorable.

UNTERMEYER, LOUIS. *American Poetry since 1900*. New York: Henry Holt, and Co., 1923, pp. 242-46. Probably the first critical appraisal of Benét aside from reviews. Contains perceptive remarks on the early poetry and notes that Benét has "sufficient power to make his future his own."

WILEY, PAUL L. "The Phaeton Symbol in *John Brown's Body*," *American Literature*, XVII (November, 1945), 231-42. First extended analysis revealing some of the depth of meaning of the epic. Scholarly and discerning, but stops short of seeing all the ramifications of its subject.

ZABEL, MORTON DAUWEN. "The American Grain," *Poetry*, XLVIII (August, 1936), 276-82. A brilliant, caustic review of *Burning City* which unjustly expands into an attack on Benét's whole poetic career as representative of the genteel "bardic" tradition. Ignores *John Brown's Body* but contains some telling strictures.

II. *Bibliographies*

The following check lists of Benét's writings and of criticism of Benét are the most nearly complete and accurate.

CHENEY, FRANCES. "Stephen Vincent Benét," in Allen Tate, ed., *Sixty American Poets, 1896-1944*. Washington: 1945, pp. 11-16. Useful for locating of copies.

JOHNSON, THOSMAS H. "Stephen Vincent Benét," in *The Literary History of the United States*, ed. Spiller, Thorp, Johnson, and Canby. New York: MacMillan, 1949, Vol. III, pp. 403-4. Short, judicious selective check list.

MADDOCKS, GLADYS LOUISE. "Stephen Vincent Benét: A Bibliography," *Bulletin of Bibliography and Dramatic Index*, (September, 1951; April, 1952), Part I, pp. 142-46; Part II, pp. 158-60. The closest approach to an exhaustive check list. Records original and subsequent printings of short stories, as well as reviews, forewords, and articles written by Benét. The omission of data concerning individual poems is the one major limitation.

Index

Abolitionists, 55
Adams, Abigail, 35
Aeneid, 46
American Dream, 83, 142, 147
American Lyric Theatre, 154
American Renaissance, 38
"American Scholar, The," 156
Anderson, Sherwood, 115
Apollo, 59
Appleseed, Johnny, 57
Appomattox Courthouse, 46
Army of Northern Virginia, 53
Army of the Potomac, 56
Army of the Tennessee, 67
Arnold, Benedict, 117
Atkinson, Brooks, 154
Atlantic Charter, 143
Austen, Jane, 138

Bacchus, 85
Barlow, Joel, 156
Barton, Clara, 35
Bathsheba, 31
Benét, Rosemary Carr, 32-34, 86-87, 90, 103, 136
Benét, Stephen Vincent: achievement, 23, 26, 28, 37, 42, 45, 46, 72, 76, 81, 97-98, 114-16, 132, 136, 143, 147-50, 151-57; Americanism, 28, 29-30, 36-37, 43, 46-48, 83, 142-44, 146, 157; ancestry, 156; boyhood, 27-28; brother, 32; career, 23, 81, 103-4, 115-16, 137-40, 144-45, 151-57; Gothic themes, 36-37; historical themes, 24-25; 26, 34, 46, 73, 103, 116-19, 127, 131, 144-46; in Paris, 29, 46-47, 87-88; interest in theatre, 154; interest in youth, 32, 34; political beliefs, 71, 137, 143, 155; realism, 72-76, 82-83, 122, 131; religious beliefs, 30-32, 32-33, 36, 84-86, 96-97, 102-3, 132, 157;

romanticism, 23, 24, 36, 72, 97, 103, 122; self-criticism, 90, 103-4, 112, 114, 115; use of folklore, 115-16, 122-24; wife, 32-34, 86-87; Yale career, 81-82, 86

WRITINGS OF:

"All Night Long," 34
America, 141-43, 151
"American Names," 28-30
"Angel Was a Yankee, The," 119
"Architects," 36
"As It Was in the Beginning," 126
"Ballad of William Sycamore, The," 27, 28-29, 30
Beginning of Wisdom, The, 31, 81-86
"Bishop's Beggar, The," 131-32
"Blood of the Martyrs, The," 130
Book of Americans, A (in collaboration with Rosemary Carr Benét), 34-36, 37
Burning City, 37-45
"By the Waters of Babylon" ("The Place of the Gods"), 125-26, 154
"Child Is Born, A," 154
"Curfew Tolls, The," 130
"Daniel Webster and the Ides of March," 116
"Daniel Webster and the Sea Serpent," 116
"Dear Adolf," 140
"Death in the Country, A," 134-36
"Devil and Daniel Webster, The," 116-19, 154, 156
"Die-Hard, The," 119
"Difference," 33
"Doc Mellhorn and the Pearly Gates," 124
Drug-Shop; or, Endymion in Edmonstown, The, 26
"Dulce Ridentem," 33-34

[169]

Index